CW00926900

ONE TO ONE,
THE ESSENCE OF RETAIL BRANDING AND DESIGN

COLOPHON

BIS Publishers
Building Het Sieraad
Postjesweg 1
1057 DT Amsterdam
The Netherlands
T +31 (0)20 515 02 30
F +31 (0)20 515 02 39
bis@bispublishers.nl
www.bispublishers.nl

ISBN 978 90 6369 264 3

Author: Michel van Tongeren, Amsterdam
michel@svt.nl
Co-author: Maaike van Rooden, Amsterdam
maaike@svt.nl
Design and illustrations: Kyra van Ineveld, Amsterdam
Translation: Mari Shields and Taalcentrum-VU, Amsterdam

retailbranding@planet.nl

ONE TO ONE
THE ESSENCE OF
RETAIL
BRANDING AND DESIGN

Michel van Tongeren

CONTENTS

PROF. RODNEY FITCH CBE

Prof. Rodney Fitch CBE, founded his design consultancy 'Fitch' in 1972. He exited the consultancy at the end of 2009 and now works in higher education and as an independent advisor, consultant and non-executive to a broad portfolio of clients.

During a distinguished career in design, Rodney has also been active in the development of design education and the arts in the UK. He was awarded a CBE in 1990 for his influence on the British design industry.

Outside of the UK he had the honour in 2005 to be inducted into the Legion of Honor and Hall of Fame of the Design Institute of America, whilst in Holland, he supervises an MA course in Retail Design at the Willem de Kooning Academy, part of the Rotterdam University of Applied Sciences and is also Professor of Retail Design at Delft University of Technology.

FOREWORD

Every year I spend a week in Arizona playing at being a cowboy. I ride the trails, herd the cattle, wear boots, spurs and a big hat. The cows and my horse carry the ranch brand, my saddle bags and bed roll carry my own – the lazy bar R. This 'branding' does not attempt to suggest any tribal, product or demographic connotations, but is a simple way of denoting ownership. If someone else has the animals or my saddle bags, they are rustlers or thieves!

Ownership and authenticity branding is many centuries old and examples can be found on items as mundane as Roman building bricks, as domestic as Chinese porcelain, to the grandeur of aristocratic heraldry.

But our contemporary involvement with brands and commercial branding is a more recent fascination and few practioners know more about the subject than Michel van Tongeren. From the emergence in the 19th Century of simple branded packaged goods to the ultra sophistication of today's brand marketing, the development, management and nurturing of brands plays a large part in commercial and cultural success. From packaging to politics; from sports to shops; from consumer goods to countries, how a brand is created, then managed and the role of design in this process is the stuff of this useful book.

Given the complexities and contradictions inherent in contemporary commercial life, what is a brand? What components, physical and psychological make it real; when does an identity become the brand; can a brand identity express a brands inner personality; how to keep a brand relevant and its reputation meaningful; do propriety brands and house brands convey more or less value to the consumer?

Brand awareness, and the relevance and trust the citizen consumer places in that brand and it's associations, is a key factor in commercial and cultural differentiation.

This is true in both a local and global context. A strong brand personality provides a stand out quality to an aspirant business in a local market, whilst it is often the brand vehicle that underpins the transformation of a successful local brand into a global one.

Furthermore and given the important lifestyle and social role retailing and shopping plays in modern life, nowhere, except perhaps in sports marketing, is the brand role more upfront and more scrutinised by the consumer. Our shopping decisions, be they for needs or wants, are most often determined by our relationship with our favourite retail brand. Increasingly where we shop and what we shop for is conditioned by the trust we place in our retailer of choice. Research shows this to be particularly so with the physical shopping experience, but the branding of the online shopping experience will likely be just as an important factor as technology drives the future shopping journey.

Michel van Tongeren knows all this. His experience in the complex world of modern branding is wide and in this book he shares his experience and advice with us. He might not know how to brand a calf, but certainly does know how to create and manage successful brands for modern commercial life – read on!

Rodney Fitch

SVT BRANDING + DESIGN GROUP

SVT Branding + Design Group was founded in 1988 by Michel van Tongeren, Joost van Santen and Laurent Vollenbregt. The company started as a multi-disciplinary design agency, but switched the field of focus to retail design, intrigued by the increased professionalism of English retail design companies. Michel now forms the management of SVT with his long time associate Frank Schoeman.

The design agency is one of the few in the Netherlands specialised in branding, strategy and the design of retail formulas. SVT develops customer environments that are a combination of the identity of the retailer, its target group and opportunities that we see in the constantly evolving society. The company is unique in the market because of the integrated approach, which combines branding, strategy, concept, design and communication with the in-depth knowledge of retail, and many years of experience in the process of brand and formula development. This comes together in a grounded and holistic retail formula design.

SVT stays driven, because every time they want to differentiate our clients from the rest. Besides the work for retailers, SVT is involved in education programs for Delft University of Technology, Utrecht Collage of The Arts and The Piet Zwart Insitute, the Masters program of The Willem de Kooning College of The Arts.

www.svt.nl

ACKNOWLEDGEMENTS

An experience. As a young boy of 17 I got my first summer job. It was immediately my first retailer experience. I worked as lift-boy at De Bijenkorf in Amsterdam. This is a world-famous department store, where in that time – as it was – the elevators were served, the departments were called and the customers were welcomed. I noticed that my colleagues, who worked there for their profession, made a fairly dull impression. If you work all day in an elevator, I understand that there is a chance that that happens. However, I was fresh, young and was excited. I was polite to the customers, but also made jokes. The fun that I had reflected on the customers, which even gave me a tip occasionally – fully against the Dutch standards.

Another experience. A few years ago I entered a Trader Joe's store in Manhattan with a group of students. It was on a Saturday at the end of the morning, and it was pleasantly busy. I didn't know Trader Joe's yet, but I had heard a lot about the concept. Although expectations were high, they were still surpassed: the atmosphere of the store, the 'alternative' approach of visual merchandising and communication, its own products and the amount of knowledge, which had been converted into nice readable information. In addition, the staff made a cheerful, interested impression. And what I noticed was that most of the customers were enjoying themselves very much, despite the fact that grocery shopping on Saturday is not the best pastime. I took many photos and the pleasant feeling did not leave me that day. Some time later I realised what had been going on there and I noticed that in other Trader Joe's stores too, that I have visited afterwards.

Both examples illustrate the universal value of life that underlie these experiences: 'love'. Love for the profession, love for what you do, and for the interaction that it yields, under the motto: "What goes around, comes around".

That sounds like a great profession, which it is. Retail is about people, about interaction and chemistry. It's about personality, genuine interest and respect. We all know examples of stupid shops, bad service and rude behaviour.

But fortunately, we know the examples of the great experience, the one-to-one contact with friendly staff, the good atmosphere in shops, the beautiful presentations or concepts that offer you so much convenience that you felt like they knew exactly what you needed that time: the ideas brought to you, which you have not thought about before, the created experience and the pleasure, that you have when you go back on the streets with filled shopping bags.

Retail is also about changing society. My tutor and friend Rodney Fitch states that 'shopping' our goal in life. He is serious about that and I understand what he means: when you get your paycheck, you do not immediately think of the insurance or redemption that you have to pay. You rather think about buying nice things. That we do mostly in physical or virtual stores, markets or perhaps in the airplane. No matter where you buy, retail it is.

This book is about that behaviour in our ever-changing society, the choices that we make, the inspiration, which seduces, and the abundances,

9

10

that make us buy. I hope you are getting excited about that. This is my second book on this subject and it is in certain way a continuation of the first, 'Retail Branding: from stopping power to shopping power'. As Jan van Buggenum, one of my friends who read the manuscript (thanks for that!), said: the first book is about how branding works and the second is about that topic too, but perhaps even more about how you can establish branding in retail.

My interest in this subject comes directly from the agency that we founded almost 25 years ago, at the same period that retail design started as a holistic profession. SVT Branding + Design Group is very experienced in the integrated process of branding and developing strategies for retailers, the development of retail formulas and designing all elements of those companies. Our ambition: to keep on surprising and inspiring the customers of our clients.

This book is made with great thanks to SVT and the people who work and have worked here in the past 25 years. They give me new insights, challenged and inspired me. My special thanks is given to Frank Schoeman, who has worked with SVT almost from the beginning, became partner and is a tower of strength: a true friend. In addition, I would personally mention Hans van de Pas. He has managed SVT from the sidelines over the last 5 years and he has kept us firmly on course.

And then Maaike Rooden. Just after I had started writing this book I was going to divorce, which was totally unexpected for me. A sad experience that took away much attention and concentration. But fortunately, Maaike continued the writing. Maaike is an experienced, ambitious brand and retail consultant. With great tenacity she has done a lot of work and research. She has ensured that the book was realised and currently lies in front of you. Thanks to her efforts, it has become very readable. I have enjoyed working with her.

I dedicate this book to my daughters Maria and Céline!

MICHEL VAN TONGEREN
Founder
Strategy & concept director
SVT Branding + Design Group

When I was little I often had a 'shop' with my brother and sister. Then we sold homemade cookies in the street and, when we were on holiday, we sold mussels we had found on the beach. On a chalk board we had written our best French: 'Moules a vendre: 1 Franc.' Our enthusiasm and the fact that we were little and cute made most sales, I think.

Now I know that there is much more to it to be a good retailer. To complete my Master's Strategic Product Design at Delft University of technology, I have dug into the retail topic. I was intrigued by the power of experiences. Which element of an experience appeals to people, what puts them in motion and how do you create a good experience? A very relevant topic for retail. Then I read 'Retail Branding: from stopping power to shopping power'. The profound way to brand and formula development appealed to me immediately. The Platform Development Model© has even formed the basis of my thesis. For me it was a logical step after graduation to apply for a job at SVT. And with success! Now, almost 5 years later, I still work with enthusiasm to the brand and formula development of our customers. I admire Michel's sharp vision and extensive knowledge about retail. I always learn from him. I find it special that the first book has motivated me to work in the retail sector and at SVT and that I got the opportunity to work on this book intensively together with Michel.

MAAIKE VAN ROODEN
Retail branding consultant
SVT Branding + Design Group

1.
DESIGN AND RETAIL DESIGN

Design as seducer

ABOUT THE INTEGRAL RELATIONSHIP WITHIN A RETAIL FORMULA, THE ROLE
AND ADDED VALUE OF DESIGN, DESIGN THINKING, THE COMBINATION OF THE
LEFT AND RIGHT BRAIN, EMOTION AND ENTREPRENEURSHIP IN RETAIL,
SEDUCING CONSUMERS AND THE CENTRAL ROLE OF THE CONSUMER.

1937

*Introduction of the first
shopping trolley, designed
by Sylvan Goldman*

1949

*Introduction shopping trolley
as we know now,
designed by Orla Watson*

■ *Poster for an open day of the Master's in Retail & Interior Design at the Willem de Kooning Academy in Rotterdam.*

TO COME STRAIGHT TO THE POINT, I AM A RETAIL DESIGNER. NO ONE, OF COURSE, IS BORN A RETAIL DESIGNER, AND UNTIL RECENTLY, IT WAS NOT POSSIBLE TO BE TRAINED TO BECOME ONE.

Retail is one of the largest, perhaps the largest sector of business in the world, but it is very little researched and hardly taught at all. Perhaps this is because the initial barriers to working in retail are so low, or because entrepreneurship and instinct, rather than academic or scientific principles, tend to predominate. It may also be because retail is a combination of so many factors and disciplines, all of which come together to become what we experience in the shops. All these factors and disciplines are united in the 'retail formula', but the knowledge that is required to build this formula cannot be captured in any single individual, and most likely not in any single course of training.

In order to be able to recognize all of these elements of retail and to develop them at the same time, someone needs to have an overall perspective, or know how to access the bigger picture. Then, like a conductor, this person needs to orchestrate the business. I sometimes compare this with the way an orchestra works, with the diversity of instruments that together create a complete, harmonious whole. To develop and manage the formula, teams in different disciplines work together, each making their contribution to the

Design gives form to the thought, so it begins with thoroughly thinking things through.

whole from the perspective of their own expertise. This is what makes retail so complex, so powerful and so interesting.

15

The harmonious connections between all the aspects of a retail formula, therefore, have to form an organic whole. Interestingly enough, the consumer in a store quickly sees these connections – or the lack thereof – between the elements. As experienced observers, consumers judge a store on the basis of the totality of impressions they experience. This experience is partly conscious and partly unconscious, and all the senses are fully alert. The consumer ultimately experiences the holistic whole, in which all the elements – from price to presentation and from personnel to service – are inextricably linked together, as a store, in the same way that we experience a symphony as a symphony, and not as a collaboration between a group of musicians. The store either 'works' or it does not, and on that basis, it will either be successful or not. This holism in retail is one of the most important themes of this book.

'TAP WATER'

0,0012

Euro per liter

CONTENT *water*
SOURCE *Belgium*
EXTRA -

**'NATURAL
MINERAL WATER'**

0,68

Euro per liter

CONTENT *water*
SOURCE *Belgium*
EXTRA *also available
in sport bottle*

THE POWER OF DESIGN

**IN ANY CASE, DESIGN IS THE STARTING
PRINCIPLE OF THIS CHAPTER. WHAT DOES
DESIGN DO?**

According to Steve Jobs, design is not just what something looks like and how it feels: design is 'how it works'. In retail design, the role of design is, I believe, to give form to the thought. With 'the thought', I mean that an idea first has to be shaped, a starting point that evolves from the brand and the strategy of the retailer. In this sense, design is the medium, with the designer as the spin doctor through whom these ambitions can ultimately be expressed. It is above all about good and careful analysis and thinking things through. On the other hand, because design gives form to the thought, design makes the distinction visible, tangible – and intangible as well – and it

> *Design is the medium and the designer is the spin doctor.*

very possibly addresses all of our senses, if the thought is a good one, that is.

Let us take water – bottled water, as an example. You can buy it in jerry cans, in bottles of one, two or three litres, or in smaller bottles. You can buy 'ordinary' water, but you can also buy the premium brands, such as SPA (€ 0.68 for 1 litre), Voss (€ 5.95 for 1 litre), or Bling H2O (with Swarovski Crystals on the bottle, at € 35 for 1 litre).

'WATER IN IT'S PUREST FORM'

5,95
Euro per liter

CONTENT *water*
SOURCE *Norway*
EXTRA *Designed by Neil Kraft, designer for Calvin Klein*

'LUXURY BOTTLED WATER'

35,00
Euro per liter

CONTENT *water*
SOURCE *Tennessee*
EXTRA *handmade bottle with Swarovski Crystal*

17

I would not dare to test them blindfolded, but if you see the bottles lined up, you can certainly attribute different values to them. Here, design clearly brings added value to a generic product and creates (brand) preference.

The importance of design has increased in a world where we are becoming more and more dependent on visual images, unlike in the past, when 'the word' played a greater role. It used to be that design and reasoning were signs of intellect. But today, we are so inundated with information, there is so much on offer around us, and we have so many decisions to make every single day, that visual images and short, rapidly digested statements are needed to get the message through to us. In this context, design has taken on enormous proportions.

If something looks appealing, we are more inclined to choose it. Design speaks to our emotions, defines our first impressions, and makes it easier for us to make a choice: it guides us in making our preliminary selection. It replaces the verbal argument, helping people to make a decision. Only after that do other aspects begin to play a role.

"Design is not just what something looks like and how it feels: design is 'how it works.'"

STEVE JOBS

DESIGN THINKING &
DESIGN DOING

MORE AND MORE, THE IMPORTANCE OF DESIGN IS BEING RECOGNIZED, AND IN RECENT YEARS, WE HAVE SEEN AN ENORMOUS INCREASE IN INTEREST IN DESIGN FROM THE BUSINESS WORLD.

Amongst other things, Tim Brown of the IDEO design studio has decisively put 'design thinking' on the map. The projects being developed by this studio, which have achieved undisputed success, have meant that the design profession is now taken seriously by the business world.

Design thinking does not necessarily mean design as such, but rather the thought process and the approach needed to achieve new insights. For our purposes, we are looking at its commercial significance. It is important in design thinking to be aware that design is not a goal in itself, but a means of achieving innovative, successful solutions. The problem is seen in its total context, and the final user or consumer is central. There is a reassessment of all the existing elements. The insights this brings are then combined with one another in a different way, in order to identify innovative, total solutions. This is not about re-examining things rigidly and rationally, because in order to identify pioneering solutions, one must avoid thinking in terms of impossibilities or strictly defined frameworks. By not looking at what the competition is doing, but acting on one's own strengths, new successes are created, instead of generic, re-engineered products.

In order to achieve this, the first thing needed is a high level of creativity. This creativity is not the

DECISION THINKING	DESIGN THINKING
• In a stable context	• In a chaotic and rapidly changing environment
• A linear approach	• A holistic approach
• Problem-oriented	• Solution focused
• Choose from existing and proven 'recipes'	• Each solution has its own unique path and own experimental way of working
• Existing situation is central	• End-user is central
• An analytical, 'ratio-scientific mode'	• A reflective, narrative and entrepreneurial mode
• Left brain	• Left and right brain

The difference between decision thinking and design thinking. A free interpretation of the list devised by Diane Nijs.

> *"We should look for next practices instead of best practices. If you focus on best practices we get copies, if you focus on next practices we are engaged in entrepeneurship."*

C.K. PRAHALAD

result of some 'high-level intellectual debate', but of an environment that allows and applauds a high degree of irrational thinking. It is not rationality, but rather intuition and emotion that bring about innovation. Rational thinking later ensures that things are practical and workable, but that comes only at a later stage.

In Change by Design, by Tim Brown, the author takes the invention and development of the light bulb by Thomas Edison as an example. Edison did not allow himself to be restricted by the limitations of what already existed. In order for his light bulb to be effectively used, he had to create a context for it. This called for the entire electricity infrastructure to be developed. Without electricity, there would be no market for its products, and therefore no commercial success for the light bulb. As we now know, this also meant the development of the electricity grid.

More recent examples include the iPhone and the iPad. To achieve them, Apple took advantage of existing technologies and media. Ease of use and design now became the central issues, so that the products could be used in highly intuitive ways. The commercial success of these products is also thanks to their extreme multifunctionality, yet people pay nothing or very little for most of the applications. These applications are easy to programme, ensuring that there is nothing to

deter potential users. Creating a new application is something that is easy to do. This made it possible for an enormous increase in applications to appear in a short time, enabling Apple to create a completely new business. This is a new form of entrepreneurship, in which people see developing a new, successful app as an exciting challenge. The result is even more growth in the use or value of the original product.

Here too, we see that it is not just a new consumer product being launched on the market, but the fact that an entire system is developed, in which that product can function. As a result, Apple, which originally began as a computer company, has grown to become the largest media company in the world. And by involving consumers themselves in developing 'the system' (the applications database), costs can be kept down, while the products themselves continue to increase in value enormously. This is the result of design thinking.

19

In fact, it can be said that design thinking takes full account of the capacities of the human brain – both halves of it. Humans have a right brain, which is specialized in such things as holistic thinking, creativity and the imagination, and is subjective. The left brain is responsible for analytical thinking, making distinctions, judgments and logic. It is this side of the brain that thinks in terms of partial problems.

Design thinking starts from a design process in which, in the first instance, the right half of the brain has free rein. Different creative techniques, such as those used in brainstorming, must enable the team to feel at ease, in order to be able to identify as many ideas as possible, which might seem completely crazy or illogical. In this phase it is all about quantity, and quality judgments do not yet play a role. This way, new solutions can be explored along untrodden paths. Only when this phase is complete does the left half of the brain come into play. Then the ideas and solutions are evaluated and, possibly, developed further.

In the Western world, logic, rational thinking and the intellect have gained the upper hand to such an extent that intuition and emotions barely still have a place. Even in the enormous commercial successes of Apple, which are actually only a result of creative thinking and design, creative techniques are still viewed with suspicion. 'Has the success of this idea already been proven by the competition?' 'Has no one else ever done it before?' 'Can you prove that it will make a profit?' These are questions that always crop up. Sometimes during a creativity exercise, one of the participants will say, 'Could I just play the devil's advocate for a moment...?'. The answer must always be, 'No. You may not play the devil's advocate, not here.' At this stage, people must not pass

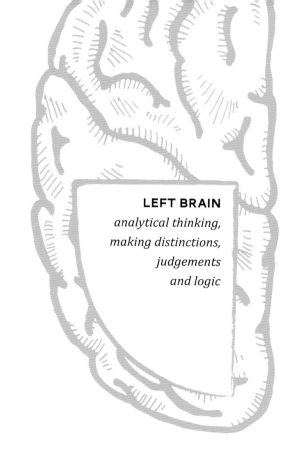

LEFT BRAIN
analytical thinking, making distinctions, judgements and logic

judgment. They must not reason logically or point out the negative implications of any idea. That would be unfortunate and foolish, because it inhibits creativity. Making judgments will be necessary in a later phase, when the still-abstract ideas have to be worked into usable concepts.

Design thinking starts from a design process in which, in first instance, the right half of the brain has free rein.

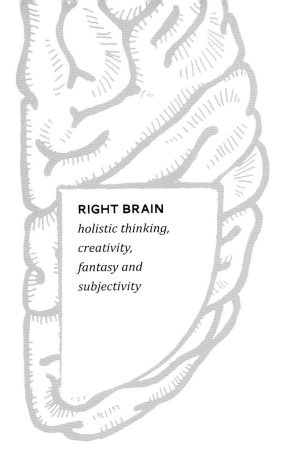

RIGHT BRAIN
*holistic thinking,
creativity,
fantasy and
subjectivity*

DESIGN THINKING IN RETAIL

IN RETAIL, THE HOLISTIC APPROACH, WHICH IS SO ESSENTIAL TO SUCCESS IN DESIGN THINKING, IS EVEN MORE SENSITIVE.

In the perception of the retailer, it is sometimes difficult to allow space for the creativity and the innovation that retail deserves and needs. Retail is already enormously complex, and it is also high-risk. Turnover is essential to ensure survival, and the effect of everything you do is immediately reflected in the cash registers. Sourcing products cheaply and offering low prices are often the rational solution used to attract customers.

In retail, it is precisely because the commercial effects of change are immediately clear that design thinking has to be an integral part of the organization, and of the brand and formula development. Successful retail design is therefore a team process, not a piece of art. For commercial retail, prima donna designers are not an option.

In an introduction to a lecture that he gave for a Master's programme in Design Management, Jos van der Zwaal aptly described what retail design is and must do:

'In modern Western society, design has become as ubiquitous as air and water. We hardly notice it anymore, confrontations with highly innovative or mind-bending examples excepted. A retail environment is the surrounding par excellence where all functionalities of design are confronted with public appreciation. Here design is challenged, tested and judged on its effectiveness without a jury, without a casebook and without mercy. The retail environment does not worry about academic divisions between graphic, interactive, product or environmental design. Here design just has to do its job. It has to be functional, physically as well as mentally. It has to communicate the targeted position and the quality level of the retailer. And it has to contribute to the reputation of the retail brand and the company behind it.'

The result has to be a store formula that is able to seduce customers into purchasing, as much as possible, as often as possible. An important tool for tempting customers is branding, which is indeed an increasingly important part of retail design. The store brand provides the input, and therefore has to ensure that the store concept has a unique and authentic character, one to which customers feel attracted. The dynamic that is

21

essential in retail, in order to continue to meet changing consumer needs, constantly demands different and new solutions, solutions that meet those needs and even surpass them.

"In the western world we are very rationally oriented and have neglected the emotional side of our existence. The coming together of these two worlds would be beneficial for the future."

GERT DUMBAR

DESIGN FOR THE CONSUMER

IN 2010, AT A LECTURE IN MUMBAI, INDIA, THE CELEBRATED DUTCH DESIGNER GERT DUMBAR ILLUSTRATED THE COMBINED EFFECT OF OUR RATIONAL AND EMOTIONAL SIDES BY JUXTAPOSING TWO DIFFERENT EXAMPLES.

The first was an illustration by Henry Dreyfuss, one of the first industrial designers, who published the book, The Measure of Man, in 1959. This book was intended to be an ergonomic reference book for designers. In one illustration, he measured the figure of man and seemed to have reduced it to an extension of the machines with which it works – the table at which he sits, the door through which he walks, and so on. The second illustration is that of the figure of man and his seven chakras. Chakra means 'wheel' in Sanskrit, and symbolizes the Vedic knowledge of our sources of energy and the spiritual life of man.

By placing these two illustrations alongside one another, Dumbar aimed to illustrate how the western world has grown to think extremely rationally, highlighting the fact that we have neglected the emotional side of our existence. In addition, he showed his Indian audience their own valuable power, a power that they could use to improve on Western limitations. By restoring the balance between the mind and the heart, the coming together of these two worlds of thought would be beneficial for the future.

In support of these ideas, one need merely point out the countless studies, research projects and books in the field of neuromarketing. This science, which is still in its infancy, has shown us that mankind is most often driven by deeply rooted emotions and urges, rather than by rational reasoning or control. Our subconscious is an efficient 'system' that seems to make its own decisions automatically.

This happens when what we are assessing or doing is not especially important, or when we have done something several times before, and it has become routine. But our unconscious is also a protection, or filter, preventing our brains from becoming unnecessarily burdened. Consciously thinking about every detail involved in all the choices that we have to make is exhausting. So instead our brains only use about 20% of the energy that they have available to them, thereby

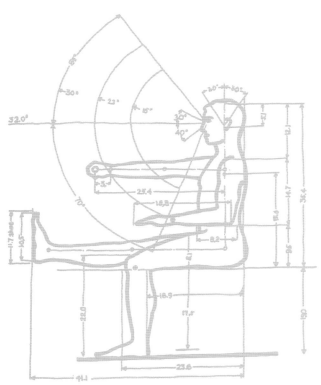

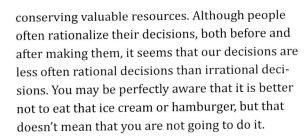

■ *The measure of man by Henry Dreyfuss.*

■ *The human being and the seven chakras.*

23

conserving valuable resources. Although people often rationalize their decisions, both before and after making them, it seems that our decisions are less often rational decisions than irrational decisions. You may be perfectly aware that it is better not to eat that ice cream or hamburger, but that doesn't mean that you are not going to do it.

This shows that the logical choices made by potential consumers are not the only things we need to consider, and that we cannot build brands solely based on their rational value. This is perhaps where the real entrepreneur comes into play, the one or ones who make and develop the brand, but who most of all feel or sense it. It is first instinct, then understanding. When people first think of design, they may first think of what we see, but we must not underestimate what we cannot see. That intangible factor makes up a large percentage of the total experience and total

assessment. It is the whole that excites the senses and determines how someone feels and behaves, and how he then judges the store or product. These influences are strong decisive factors in determining purchasing behaviour and the experience of the store, and they often have a far greater effect than initially anticipated. When consumers attribute value to a store formula, the right half of their brains plays a crucial role, and this again explains how consumers can perceive it entirely holistically, recognize when one or more elements do not work properly, or indeed, that they all feel completely as they should.

2.
THE ESSENCE OF RETAIL

The one to one relationship

ABOUT THE DAILY DRUDGERY FACED BY RETAILERS, ABOUT THE SEDUCTION OF INDIVIDUAL SHOPPERS, RESPONDING TO CONSUMER NEEDS, THE RELATIONSHIP BETWEEN RETAILER AND CUSTOMER, RELEVANCE FOR THE INDIVIDUAL AND THE RETAILER'S RIGHT TO EXIST, THE DIFFERENCE BETWEEN THE MASS MEDIA AND IN-STORE COMMUNICATIONS, RETAIL AS THE MIRROR OF SOCIETY, THE ORIGINS OF MARKETING, THE INFLUENCE OF THE INTERNET, THE CUSTOMER IN THE DRIVING SEAT, INTERACTION IN RETAIL 3.0 AND WHY EVERYTHING IS BECOMING RETAILIZED.

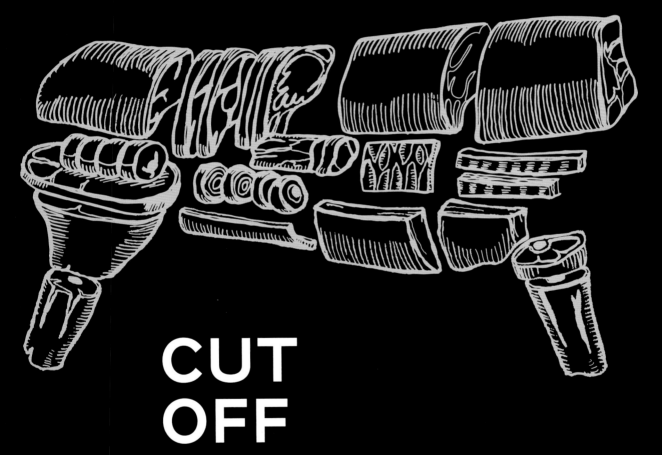

CUT
OFF

The word retail comes from the French word, retailler or 'to cut again'.

■ *The personal relationship between customer and retailer was once obvious.*

A ONE TO ONE RELATIONSHIP

THE WORD RETAIL COMES FROM THE FRENCH WORD, RETAILLER, OR 'TO CUT AGAIN'. THE IDEA IS THAT THE SHOP-KEEPER PURCHASES AN ENTIRE SAUSAGE. HE THEN CUTS OFF SLICES FOR US AND SELLS THEM TO US BY THE OUNCE.

The whole sausage would be too big and too expensive for individual buyers, and the increased ease or comfort is a service to the customers. For the initial investment, for keeping the product cool, for slicing and packaging it for each individual customer, the retailer can ultimately ask more money than what he actually paid for the sausage. In Dutch, this is called *detailhandel*, or 'detail trade': people purchase in bulk and sell 'in detail'. Regardless of whether the shop turns over 1 million or 1 billion, the retailer still has to bring

in a certain amount each day, or for each transaction, or from each individual purchaser. Together, these small amounts ultimately make up a large annual turnover. This 'per transaction' activity highlights the drudgery of the retailer's day-to-day labour. Every day, over and over again, the retailer has to make relevant propositions to individual shoppers, in order to convince them to buy. This calls for considerable knowledge about the individual needs of that customer. Insight into the relationship between the retailer and the consumer is also essential. Retail is therefore not so much about shops and shopping centres, but about the one-to-one relationships between companies and real people, in which the company becomes a person and the encounter the equivalent of a conversation.

27

Retail is not so much about shops and shopping centres, but about the one-to-one relationship between companies and real people, in which the company becomes a person and the encounter the equivalent of a conversation.

Because almost all transactions are individual transactions, all communications about them are aimed at the individual and are relevant within their own specific context. This one-to-one communication is the essential difference between what is communicated through the mass media and how the retailer behaves in the shop. Mass media communications aim to attract people's attention, enticing them into the shops. Once they are there, both the message and what is being offered for purchase, the available supply, have to be made interesting: the personal advantages have to be clearly illustrated to those individual buyers.

As an example, a Dutch bank placed large posters along the highways, with the words, 'How much money do you actually have?' For the mass media,

it is a good turn of phrase, one that gets people thinking and might even tempt them to go into their banks for a chat. Once that customer was 'in the store', in a personal, one-to-one encounter, that question would be considered improper, at least in the Netherlands. In this case, one then has to come up with a modified version, a relevant translation of the mass media question. It might then become, 'What is your spending limit?' or, 'Shall we take a look at what you actually have and see whether or not it is enough for your pension,' or something of that nature.

You market to the masses, but sell to individuals.

IKEA's Anna helps the customer online with all his questions.

INFLUENCED BY A CHANGING WORLD

IN ORDER TO MAKE THAT ONE-TO-ONE RE-LATIONSHIP A VALUABLE ONE, TIME AND TIME AGAIN, THE RETAILER HAS TO KNOW WHAT IS GOING ON IN THE MINDS OF CONSUMERS, AND IN SOCIETY AT LARGE.

He then needs to act accordingly: translate what he sees into their relationship in order to ensure that it remains intact, or is even improved. In this sense, retail is something organic: it shifts and transforms along with the changes in the world. But retail can also change the world. We can say that there is a continuous exchange between our ever-changing society and the changes in retail, sometimes triggered by the one, sometimes by the other, yet always communicating. Retail is the mirror of society. We all know lots of examples of independent shops and chain stores that have become irrelevant, that can no longer keep up with changing society, that fail to anticipate these changes and have therefore lost their right to exist. Everlasting customer loyalty does not exist. Consumers will remain a retailer's customers only until they are offered a better, more pleasant, cheaper or otherwise advantageous alternative.

How does the world change? Why is the world continuously changing? Does the world change on its own; is it driven by its own forces or does it change under the influence of people, in response to our needs, fears and ambitions? When there are really big changes, too large for us to understand how they result from the individual desires and drives of people, then we can say that the world changes on its own. This can happen because of natural disasters, or through wars, terrorism, massive increases in prosperity or something of this kind – in any case, major factors. Of course we could say that 8 out of 10 changes are the results of human actions. Some even say that global warming and a large percentage of these natural disasters are ultimately down to us. Nonetheless, all of this takes place on such a large scale that it is very difficult for us to attribute the changing world to changes in the needs or behaviour of people, or indeed consumers.

In any case, if we look at the developments of recent years, we can see a rapid succession of events that clearly affected our everyday lives. Globalization has given us a completely different view of the world. Although the term globalization had already existed for a long time, its modern definition has largely been attributed to Theodore Levitt. This modern form of globalization applies principally to the worldwide process that brings different societies, cultures and economies together as a result of technological developments, in cheaper forms of transport and in information and communication technology. The result is in an enormous expansion in scale, which is spreading the mentality of the western world, capitalism and consumerism around the globe, reshaping the world into a simpler form.

29

> *There is a continuous exchange between our ever-changing society and the changes in retail, sometimes triggered by one, sometimes by the other, yet always communicating.*

Small stores with local relevance are gaining in popularity. This is the Dutch supermarket Marqt, which stocks only organic, local and seasonal products.

On the one hand, people are also seeing the benefits. Life is becoming easier. The internet is fun, there are countless TV channels, and so on. On the other hand, the world has become more transparent and extremely large, and this has led to irreversible consequences. We have witnessed the growth of the internet, which later burst apart with the 1995-2000 internet bubble, the destruction of the Twin Towers in New York City in 2001, the enormous economic growth in the West between 2004 and 2008, the rise of the BRIC countries, notably China and India, and the economic crisis, beginning with the banking crisis of 2008. We know that all of these events were the result of human actions. For each of us personally, however, it goes over our heads. People feel that individually, they are just a tiny little spoke in this enormous wheel. As a result, they begin to doubt their personal situations, which they seem to have less and less under control, and many people are inclined to withdraw into their own, more personal territories, in an effort to make the world a little bit smaller and more manageable again.

Standing inside all of these developments and influences is the individual, the one being tossed back and forth, between future and past, between a modern world and a yearning for the nostalgic security and comfort of earlier times. The consequence of all this doubt is unpredictable, contradictory behaviour. This is expressed, for example, in such developments as traditionalism, fundamentalism, terrorism, nationalism and patriotism. One reaction in the retail world is that smaller shops, with greater local relevance, are gaining more and more popularity compared to the big, anonymous chains. In the food sector, people are

RETAIL IS THE MIRROR OF SOCIETY

31

increasingly using seasonal products sourced from local farmers, saving energy on production and distribution and boosting local regions at the same time.

People have also become more afraid of terrorist threats in public places, and a new version of 'cocooning' has evolved, with people preferring to meet with their friends at home. In response to this need, professional machines, including beer taps and coffee espresso machines, have been 'translated' into machines for household use. On the other hand, we could no longer do without the new possibilities that globalization has brought us, nor would we want to. Just imagine what the world would be like without the internet. We would no longer have such easy and rapid access to so much information, no longer be able to shop 24 hours a day, seven days a week, no longer have the contacts with the outside world that social media now make possible.

ONE TO ONE CUSTOMER CONTACT

BEFORE THE PHENOMENON OF LARGE-SCALE SHOPPING, PRODUCTS WERE DELIVERED 'IN PERSON', DIRECTLY BY THE FARMERS THEMSELVES, OR BY VENDORS OR LOCAL MARKETS.

Shoes came from cobblers, clothes from tailors and seamstresses, bread from the baker. There was individual, personal contact and interaction between those purchasing and those selling – at least during the transaction itself. Frequently, the products or services being requested or provided were specially tailored to meet the specific needs of the customer and, of course, the particular

professional skills of the supplier. Depending on the consumer's needs, that consumer went to whichever artisan was best able to meet his bespoke requirements.

Here, marketing did not yet play an official role, but it evolved when more than one artisan in the same craft became available in the same neighbourhood, so that they competed with one another. At this point, the different, the distinctive qualities of each were played against one another, in order to bring the supplier, the product or the service to the attention of the potential customers, hopefully securing a place for that

■ *Through the knowledge it gains of its customers through the Nespresso Club, Nespresso can address them personally.*

Physical retail will have to learn from the possibilities being offered by the internet and find clever ways of integrating these insights.

particular source as the favourite in those customers' minds. If one considers marketing as a way of thinking and acting, it has probably always, in certain way, been a factor in bringing materials and services to customers. In this context, marketing can be defined as the illustration of certain specifications of products and services, coupled with the identity of the supplier or producer. These qualities have to connect to the needs of the consumer. For that consumer, it is always about the relevance and the context of what is being offered, and about the distinctive qualities of the supplier, so that particular supplier stands out, and is selected by the consumer.

In the time that has elapsed between this one-to-one exchange and today, under all kinds of influences, an enormous increase in scale has taken place and the personal sale of mass-produced products has largely disappeared, making way for increasingly anonymous transactions. Mass-produced goods are manufactured by more efficient processes. The consequence of this is that the selling process also needs to become more efficient. To a large degree, advertising has taken over the personal role of the supplier. The supplier is no longer personally present at

the transaction, and certainly cannot be everywhere at once. For this reason, other means have had to be found in order to communicate the relevance, the context and the distinctive qualities of the particular supplier.

Here, it probably went largely unnoticed that the role of the customer also changed, as he also became a part of the buying process. For example, when someone shops at a supermarket, it is the customer, who is the 'order picker', rather than the shop employee. When you withdraw money from an ATM, you are replacing the bank employee. These processes have long ceased to involve any personal contact or even the simple acknowledgement of the individual customer. Although people sometimes still complain about the anonymity of shopping, it has become an accepted part of life. One even wonders if people would want to stand in the queue at the bakery, the butcher shop or the bank. The speed of our daily lives calls for new methods and resorting to the old ways is no longer an option. Yet we still retain a nostalgic longing for the old and familiar, and we see this desire returning in the form of a method or a style, if not in actual fact.

33

One interesting development is that the internet and mobile technology are enabling a totally new form of one-to-one customer contact. The customer is now approached online, in his own environment. When someone has set up a profile on a website, they are approached by name, or perhaps by their username. Their previous visits can be referred to and proactive offers presented, suited to their own personal preferences. In addition, based on someone's internet search behaviour, recommendations can be made and products displayed that other people with similar profiles have looked for. These people become a kind of anonymous peer group, and this can be used to inspire yet more people. In addition, it is very easy to consult friends or strangers for tips and opinions before deciding to buy. When this happens, the tone is more personal, and customers also experience this communication – paradoxically enough, as this communication is computer generated – as a warmer contact than contact in a physical shop, where real people work, but where people do not know you and therefore, in most cases, are unaware of your personal profile.

This is not about competition between the virtual store and the physical store. It is about the insight that is provided by their responding to different demands and reinforcing one another in order to satisfy the customers' needs during the selling process. This new process of search and find, the personal approach and the ease of online and mobile shopping all need to be recreated in the physical world. Where desirable, contact with the customer needs to be reinforced or replaced by new methodologies. It is possible that the role of the employee will also change as a result, and internet technology, together with all the mobile forms it takes, will continue to be further developed and refined. In this context, retailers must increasingly transform to suit the desires of his consumers, because thanks to the wide range of possibilities, it is now the customers who are more often in the driving seat, and it is the customers who will fulfil an ever greater role in the process of seeking, purchasing and fulfilling their desires.

Real insight into the desires of the individual customers is therefore of essential importance, because only by anticipating these can value be created and the one-to-one relationship reinforced. The products and the services also have to be relevant in the context in which they are being offered. This context includes both the (selling) environment and the sense of timing on the part of the shop, whether this is a physical or a virtual shop. It is also the context in which the product or service being offered is going to be used. All of this in turn exists within the framework of a changing world and changing needs.

Here lies an important task for retailers. They must engage in interaction with their customers to help them make their choices, because the world is already complex enough, and there is ever greater choice, thanks to all the possibilities of the Western world. Through the insights that evolve from this interaction, there will be a better match between supply and demand, and supply will increasingly be determined by the consumer. Within this setting, physical retail must find a new role and a new form, which connect to the changing world and changing needs. Physical retail will have to learn from the possibilities being offered by the internet and find clever ways of integrating these insights.

THE VIRTUAL AND PHYSICAL MUST INTERACT

EVERYTHING BECOMES RETAIL

AS A RETAILER, TO RETAIN THE RIGHT TO EXIST, IT IS ESSENTIAL TO NURTURE THE RELATIONSHIP WITH CONSUMERS AND ADAPT TO CONSUMERS' SHIFTING INDIVIDUAL NEEDS.

Analysing that consumer and the world he lives in has therefore evolved into an advanced and deeply rooted discipline, practised by retailers, either by means of scientific methods or on the basis of entrepreneurship and gut feelings. Strong retail organizations – those that will survive in the long run – have mastered the art of interpreting the products they offer the masses into the individual people within the individual store. Only if you engage in personal conversations with individual customers and can appeal to them inside the shop will they have positive memories of you, and choose to come back to you in the future.

It is a well-known saying: 'The customer is king.' It is also an increasingly stark reality for the retailer. The abundance of choices available to consumers and their increasing options for sharing information amongst themselves make it necessary for retailers to serve their customers at all times, catering to those customers' needs and desires. The brand is therefore slowly but surely no longer the property of the distributor, manufacturer or retailer, but also of the market. The consumer may act as ambassador for a brand, but he can also undermine it. Interaction between the supplier and the customer will continue to be a necessary part of the equation.

36

The right to exist depends on the relationship with consumers and adapting to their shifting needs.

Because the consumer is assuming an increasingly powerful position, I believe that all brands will have to create and maintain a one-to-one relationship with their customers. The supplier must create a persona for itself and ensure this maintains its position in the marketplace. In order to do this, the identity of the supplier and the behaviour associated with that identity has to be recognizable, consistent and desirable. This has repercussions for how total identities will need to be developed in the future and how these are presented to the world. To succeed, this calls for deeply-rooted knowledge of the brand identity and of the entire playing field in which the brand has a presence. This principle is central to this book.

The waiting room at the Chamber of Commerce in Amsterdam used to be somewhere just for waiting. Now it is a dynamic hub, where entrepreneurs can meet, arrange their affairs and access all the information they need, self-service or full service.

As indicated, the one-to-one relationship in retail is a centuries-old principle that has to be continually kept up to date. This success in fulfilling individual needs has its source in the competitive nature of the retail world. It is a battle amongst retailers that can only be won through the power to attract and entice and appealing to consumers by offering something that is relevant and pertinent to them. This principle and the knowledge that it creates are also valuable to nonretail channels, and for that reason will be picked up in more and more places, especially in the care and service sectors. Here too, institutions are also facing increasing competition and can only survive if they are, and continue to be, the first choice for their clients. To do this, they have to do better than just meeting these clients halfway. The essence of resale – one-to-one customer contact – will continue to spread its influence ever wider. In other words, everything is becoming retail.

Charities and medical institutions are using retail to gain direct contact with people. Above: a British Heart Foundation store. Below: a French doctors' shopping bag with direct contact details.

Right: As with many banks in the Western world, ABN-AMRO Bank offers customers an inviting retail concept where equality between customers and bank staff is paramount. (Artist's impression by Sinot Branding & Design)

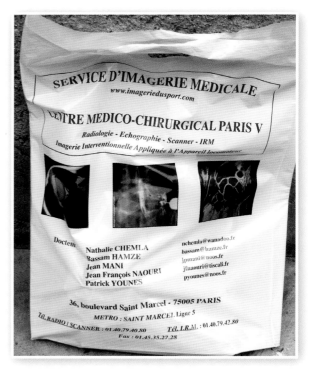

EVERYTHING
IS BECOMING
RETAILIZED

RETAIL 3.0: THE CUSTOMER DECIDES

THE FACT THAT INTERACTION WITH THE CONSUMER IS INCREASINGLY IMPORTANT, THAT THE CONSUMER'S DESIRES AND NEEDS ARE INCREASINGLY WHAT DECIDE THINGS, WAS APTLY ILLUSTRATED IN A 2009 ARTICLE BY HAWKINS STRATEGIC LLC, A MARKETING CONSULTANCY NEAR SYRACUSE, NY, USA. THE ARTICLE OUTLINES THE STEPS THAT RETAIL MARKETING HAS UNDERGONE AND IS STILL UNDERGOING.

The first step highlighted in the article is that, in America, thanks to the rise of nationwide television, it became possible for major manufacturers to efficiently and effectively reach very broad audiences. This was made possible by this popular medium, which at the time only had a few broadcasting channels. This development is nicely illustrated in the HBO series, Mad Men. Thanks to the enormous revenues that this generated, manufacturers were able to invest in consumer research, direct-to-consumer sales campaigns and nationwide advertising. These companies helped make the marketplace more scientific. Stores came to be seen as distribution points for their products. The power in the supply chain was in the hands of the manufacturers: Retail 1.0.

The mid-1990s saw two striking new trends, which brought things to a turning point. One was a consolidation on the parts of retailers of fast-moving consumer goods. A strong example of this was Wal-Mart, which also began retailing food. The result was that there were fewer retailers, but they were notably very large retailers, and they capitalised on their massive purchasing power with the manufacturers. With this development came the rise of the individual brand, which also took on the competition with manufacturers. The other important trend was the development and rapid growth of loyalty programmes. Whether or not these programmes actually worked is not so much the issue, and is subject to debate, but the enormous accumulation of data and client information that came into the hands of retailers, combined with the consolidation, made them stronger than ever. It was a shift of power from the manufacturers to the retailers. They were, of course, the ones who had direct contact with the customers, something that the manufacturers lacked: Retail 2.0.

Today, we are witnessing the beginning of the development of Retail 3.0, in which the individual shopper will at last be the one holding the power. In the article, Hawkins makes a strong argument for the value of knowledge of the individual shopper and the specific supply chain. The motto is 'Know your customer.' Next, it is a question of linking what you have to offer to the personal needs of that customer: it is a form of mass customization. Customers also want to be approached on a personal level and traditional mass media communications are proving increasingly less effective in reaching out to customers.

Advertising seems incapable of properly conveying the unique message, and the personal touch is lost in the anonymity of the major companies, the originators of the message.

The reach of traditional media is also declining as a result of a changing media landscape. Because of the rise of the internet and all the ways that it can be used, it has become diverse and broad in scope. Traditional channels have to share the marketplace with these new forms, and they are even being used simultaneously: we watch television with a laptop in our laps; we have digital, interactive TV, online TV and a smartphone. Advertising in traditional media alone has less effect, but as a result, there are now tremendous opportunities for more targeted communications, tailored and directed to the individual, enabling the various media to be used to complement one another.

41

RETAIL 1.0
THE POWER IS IN HANDS OF THE MANUFACTURER

RETAIL 2.0
THE POWER IS IN HANDS OF THE RETAILER

RETAIL 3.0
THE POWER IS IN HANDS OF THE CONSUMER

3.
RETAIL PLATFORM DEVELOPMENT MODEL©

*The holistic approach of retail branding
and formula development*

ABOUT THE RETAIL FORMULA IN ITS CONTEXT, THE HOLISTIC COHERENCE BETWEEN THE CHANGING WORLD, CONSUMERS AND RETAILERS, ABOUT WHAT A RETAILER CAN AND CANNOT INFLUENCE AND HOW THE PLATFORM DEVELOPMENT MODEL© WORKS.

VERSE 11

"We put thirty spokes together and call it a wheel,
but it is on the space where there is nothing,
that the usefulness of the wheel depends."

44

■ *Retailers aim to transform the masses into customers, step by step. A multitude of signs in an Amsterdam shopping street.*

VERSE 11 OF TAO TE CHING

We put thirty spokes together and call it a wheel;

But it is on the space where there is nothing

that the usefulness of the wheel depends.

We turn clay to make a vessel;

But it is on the space where there is nothing

that the usefulness of the vessel depends.

We pierce doors and windows to make a house;

And it is on these spaces where there is nothing

that the usefulness of the house depends.

Therefore just as we take advantage of what is,

we should recognize the usefulness of what is not.

IN ORDER TO REALIZE THE ESSENTIAL RELATIONSHIP WITH CONSUMERS, IT IS IMPORTANT TO UNDERSTAND THE ENTIRE RETAIL PLAYING FIELD.

What do they enjoy and what do they worry about? As a retailer, you need to have knowledge of this and act accordingly, because the retailer's ultimate goal is to attract the attention of consumers and turn lookers into buyers. The retailer must be very aware of how he can attract and entice consumers, in order to then get them to buy something and ultimately build up a relationship with them, so that they come back.

A retail formula can therefore only be successful if we are able to make this connection with the market and with the individual needs of consumers.

To create this one-to-one relationship, it is crucial to have knowledge of one's own brands and the constantly changing environment in which the retail formula and our customers exist. Change sometimes starts with the changing world, but it sometimes begins with consumers. It is sometimes the outside world, but sometimes it is the retailer with an original concept who changes consumer behaviour. New techniques and other innovations can also play a major role.

The Platform Development Model© is an effective and useful tool. At a glance, it offers insight into the different forces that play a role in retail. It shows the holistic coherence of retail, which means that the different layers and segments of the model are all closely interwoven and continue to affect one another.

Verse 11 of the ancient Laozi Tao Te Ching gives a beautiful description of holism, of the need for the visible and the invisible to work together. They complement one another, and both are necessary to achieve the end result.

The holistic interplay between what we see and what we do not see also applies to retail. Every brand is made up of a rational side, the company values and conditions, and an emotional side, which is the DNA of the enterprise. The Platform Development Model© makes it possible for us to see into these interrelationships, as a kind of wheel with the brand as the hub.

The outermost rings of the model represent the external forces, the context. They are the changing world, consumers and their behaviours, which can be different in different circumstances and situations. The inner sections are the internal forces: the brand and the formula. Both parts of this model come together in the customer journey. This is the contact, the relationship between the consumer and the retailer, in all its forms and at all its locations, physical or virtual, from first contact to purchase, and we must never forget what happens after that purchase takes place.

With this model, all of the retail elements that together make up the formula can be developed, redeveloped and tracked, as people can now anticipate changes that come from outside. Because of its holistic character, the model can be used from the inside out or from the outside in. Change sometimes begins with the outside world, sometimes with the retailer. Sometimes the world we live in is changed by the needs and desires of consumers and sometimes the world changes those consumers. It is all rather difficult to pin down or predict: we have to remain vigilant.

EXTERNAL FORCES: THE CONTEXT

WE BEGIN HERE WITH THE OUTSIDE OF THE WHEEL, WHICH CHARTS THE INFLUENCES FROM EXTERNAL FACTORS. IN PRINCIPLE, THESE ARE ELEMENTS ON WHICH RETAILERS HAVE NO DIRECT INFLUENCE, BUT TO WHICH THEY MUST RESPOND.

The outer ring of the model describes our changing world. The never-ending dynamics of society mean, amongst other things, that the environments in which we live are constantly changing their appearance. These may be forces that we cannot directly affect, but they still influence our attitudes in society. To a greater or lesser degree, this in turn influences our needs, the way we shop and our brand preferences.

Then there are the consumers, who have or who acquire different needs, who go along with the spirit of their times and the constraints of time. Within this category, they are again subject to situations, emotions or moments that determine or influence their behaviour. This means that one and the same person can become a different customer in different circumstances, with different needs on each occasion. A man can be spoken to in his role as a father, but also as a member of his circle of friends, or as his mother's son. Take, for example, an international businessman, who travels business class and stays at four-star hotels. If he takes a holiday in the sun for a week with his family, he might well travel economy class and stay in a three-star hotel. If he decides to go to London for a weekend with his mates, he might fly with a low-cost carrier and sleep in a budget hotel, because they are not doing much sleeping anyway.

The consumer is anything but a static individual, but a person who operates within a whole range of situations, who belongs to different groups and plays a different role within each group. This dynamic is a determining factor and makes it difficult to isolate consistent patterns in consumer behaviour. For this reason, segmentation

47

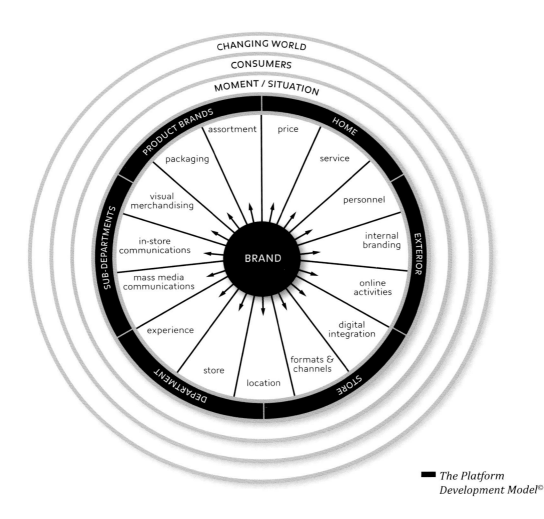

The Platform Development Model©

according to demographic factors is no longer much use. Instead, we need insight into different situations and behaviours.

These diverse possibilities, changes and behaviours clearly have a tremendous impact on retail. The interaction between the changing and changed world and consumer behaviour makes it more complex for a retailer to fully grasp external circumstances, because the world is growing smaller, faster and more dynamic. It is therefore important to gain an understanding of the broad contours and to place developments into their proper perspective and context. Here lie countless opportunities for gaining the advantage over competitors and for surprising potential customers with things that seamlessly connect to their own changing needs and desires.

There are different techniques and models that can help in gaining such insight into this backdrop. Time and experience will reveal which techniques work best for any given enterprise. We have included several of these techniques here.

The SWOT (Strengths, Weaknesses, Opportunities, Threats) analysis is helpful in charting developments in the marketplace. At a brainstorming session, people discuss the relevance and the impact of developments, both positive and negative, on their market and on their organization. By then linking these with the strengths and weaknesses of the organization, the internal analysis, strategies can be devised to enable the organization to respond to the external influences.

In addition to knowing about the developments in society, it is important to know the competition, the wider field in which we are operating. This can be tracked by means of a positioning diagram, in which two axes are set against one another using the relevant values of choice. For supermarkets, for example, this could be level of service and value for money. In this diagram, the various competitors are tracked by assessing them against these values. The degree to which they satisfy them determines their place in the diagram. This gives an overall picture of where an organization stands in terms of these values and in relationship to other players. Based on this overview, directions for further development can be determined – where there is a gap in the market and which values should be emphasized.

One useful aid or filter in charting the competition is to analyse the various players based on their positioning principles. This is the factor that is central to the profiling of any brand. By applying this filter, insight into the competition is enhanced, so that parties striving for the same objectives can be compared. In their book, Positioneren (Positioning), Rik Riezenbos and Jaap van der Grinten identify four basic categories of positioning that focus on the organization's core objectives, the product, the marketing variables or the recipient.

These techniques for exploring the competition focus primarily on current conditions. However, Porter's Five Forces Analysis offers more insight into possible influences in the longer term. According to Michael Porter, the five forces at work in competition include direct competition,

MOST FORMULAS IN RETAILING ARE SIMPLE, IT'S KEEPING THEM UP DAY TO DAY THAT IS DIFFICULT

GORDON SEAGULL, FOUNDER CRATE & BARREL

purchasing power, supplier power, the threat of new participants and the degree to which substitutes are available or possible. This technique compels an organization to think about what might happen and what the consequences might be if a new player appears suddenly and unexpectedly.

In addition to knowing about developments in society and amongst the competitors, knowing the effects that these factors have on consumers is every bit as important. After all, they are ultimately the ones who have to (continue to) visit the store. Through consumer analyses, it is possible to gain a picture of consumer needs, how they spend their time and why they choose certain retailers.

It is important to determine in advance exactly what information is needed and what research techniques are most suitable. In most cases, a combination of qualitative and quantitative research is advisable, because this ensures that results are supported by large numbers of people and makes it possible to examine certain subjects in greater detail with a smaller group, so that more specific knowledge and details can be collected.

A healthy dose of common sense is needed when analysing a context. Here, instinct and entrepreneurship are important, because models are always a simplified and more static representation of reality. The insights that they generate need to be translated into usable data to develop and update the retail formula.

THE RETAIL CHOICE DIAGRAM©

BETWEEN THE OUTSIDE RINGS AND THE ACTUAL STORE FORMULA, IS THE CUSTOMER JOURNEY.

This embraces all the steps that customers have to go through, and all of the choices they face, from first encountering a brand to the purchase of a product in a physical or virtual store. It begins with a (latent) need, with the creation of a mental shortlist, which includes the store or stores to be visited, and actually going there. Then, once in the store, there is the trajectory from outside the store, through the store to the section where they will have to decide, yes or no. During this entire process, the retailer needs to guide the consumers, help them make choices and continue to appeal to them as they approach the formula, enter and decide whether to make a purchase. This has to be a continuous chain, so that the retailer and the consumer are connected to one another in a bond that becomes increasingly closer and more personal as the customer journey progresses. To do this, to ensure that the consumer remains enthusiastic, the retailer has to communicate a relevant message at every point along the way, a message that suits the consumer's interest and focus at that specific moment, with the aim that he becomes a customer.

This is no easy task, given that every consumer is a dynamic individual and that the process of seeking and purchasing is becoming more and more multifaceted. Today, consumers have to make choices based on new and different considerations, and they can consult different media to better orientate themselves and actually decide to purchase something. Nonetheless, it can be said that the considerations and the choices that

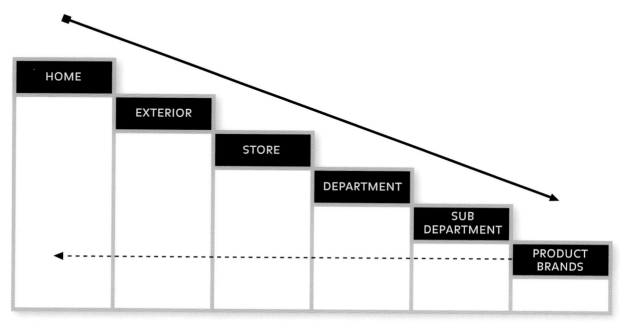

The Retail Choice Diagram©

play a part in the different phases of the purchasing process in fact apply both to physical stores, for which people must leave their homes or places of business to actually go to the store, and to webshops, where the homepage has to be located and visited before one moves on to specific products and a possible purchase.

A retailer must communicate a relevant message at every point of the customer journey.

■ *What should you choose in the jewellery department? Seduction is everywhere in this shop in Singapore.*

INTERNAL FORCES:
BRAND AND FORMULA

THE INNER SECTION OF THE MODEL CONCERNS THE ORGANIZATION: FORMULA DEVELOPMENT AND FORMULA MANAGEMENT. IT ALLOWS US TO SEE THE TOTAL COHERENCE OF BRAND, MARKETING MIX AND RETAIL FORMULA IN A HOLISTIC MANNER.

Within organizations, people are generally inclined to split a store formula into digestible parts or disciplines, so that they can be delegated to different internal and/or external parties. This may indeed produce a more transparent, rectilinear process and clearer assignments, but it clouds the overview of the process as a whole. It can also lead to the different sections each taking on a life of its own, causing a breakdown of cohesion. We have to learn to live with this paradox, learn to unravel the complexity of the formula, while at the same time continuing to see the formula as a whole.

At the very heart of the Platform Development Model© is the brand. This is made up of its DNA, the essence of the brand, its position in relation to the competition and the ambitions of the enterprise, or in other words, the vision of the brand, the brand's market and the brand's future. Ambition is an inseparable part of this and the driving force of the brand, but at the same time, it also creates a boundary. This is what everyone must work towards. The outer circumference here is the retail concept, the imaginary but ultimately also the physical and virtual container of the formula. In the model, the brand is used as an instrument for making the implicit identity and values of the organization explicit. In this way, it serves as a guideline for the development of the store concept. The result has to be a store concept whose every part communicates the brand.

In this model, the parts of the formula, known as the marketing mix, lie within the circle of the retail concept and come together at the centre, the brand. This means that the elements can be directed and guided from the centre, and work together. In developing the retail concept, all the parts of the formula are important. The idea is that during the development of the formula, the parts are filled in completely and in relation to one another. If, for example, you have everything all organized, but the assortment is not good, you are too expensive or your staff does not understand the formula or the brand, then you do not have a viable store. Everything has to be right. This is because consumers have become experts in understanding brands, stores and the signals inherent to them. At a glance, they know whether it all works or not. The model is therefore both a holistic development platform and a launch platform. Timing plays a major role: all the elements have to be right before a launch can take place.

The outer circumference of the internal part of the model is the retail concept, the imaginary, but ultimately also the physical and virtual container of the formula.

The reason for doing things this way is that consumers also experience a brand and a formula in the same way in both its physical and its virtual form. In contrast to manufacturing, for example, in retail, the entire company is immediately visible, whether it is about ambience, assortment, price, staff (their appearance, as well as how they act). It is what it is: there is no opportunity to suddenly present a brand differently.

As an example, let us look at a manufacturer, such as Mars. If they want to develop a new candy bar and aim to generate the hippest hype, they have a good chance of success. They develop the recipe and the programme, have an attractive wrapping designed, choose a 'fancy' advertising company and pour millions into the ad campaign. With the right qualities put into each of these steps, it is possible for them to launch the hippest candy bar onto the marketplace. That is because their customers never enter the factory grounds and therefore never see that there are just ordinary people working there, the same people who produce Mars bars, M&Ms and Bounty, as well as this new, ultra-hip candy bar. The new product stands independently and is able to lead a life of its own.

In retail, this is not possible. There is nowhere to hide. Customers experience the whole operation all at once. They see the products, experience the ambience, know whether the relationship between quality and price is right or not, whether the staff understand and so on. In short, if you want to be the hippest in retail, you really have to be the hippest. For that reason, the store formula, in all of its aspects, has to be in line with the brand and be properly developed within its potential bandwidth.

If you want to be the hippest in retail, you really have to be the hippest.

Because brand authenticity is needed, it is essential to reveal the real character of the enterprise, to make it tangible, something people can talk about, and then, from the perspective of this knowledge, chart new courses. Only in this way can a truly genuine and unique brand be developed. Indeed, these new objectives and trajectories have to be refined and enhanced by being tested in context. The interchange between brands and the outer rings of the model ensure that the store ultimately makes and keeps its connection with consumers.

THE BRAND

As we have said, this is a holistic model. There is in fact no hierarchy at all, beyond the brand that generates the formula. For this reason, everyone who influences the elements of the formula (initiators, leaders, etc.) has to be connected to the core. This in any case includes the brand owner, the directors, the brand manager and/or the (perhaps external) 'brand team'.

The essence of the brand provides a base on which to develop the formula. It is therefore important to have a good description of the brand, to properly record that description and interpret it in terms of behavioural guidelines. In this way, agreement is reached throughout the entire organization and the entire organization can act based on the essence of the brand. It is also important, during the entire quest, that the words used to express the essence of the brand are also visually illustrated. For example, if someone uses the word 'chic', others have to understand what that person understands as 'chic'. Visual images, symbols and mood boards play an important role in keeping everyone on the same page. Combined with the words, these images are also important in making clear to those who were not present in the process what people really mean, where it is intended to lead and how it might look.

PARTS OF THE FORMULA

The different formula parts in the Platform Development Model© are based on the marketing mix, but this mix is not (necessarily) complete. It can be adapted or supplemented as needed. Figure 1a shows the formula parts that will all (at a given time) have to pass muster. The parts do not stand on their own, but together form a whole, although which are most important can vary from one retail formula to another. Logically speaking, it is convenient to tackle those more important aspects first, but in fact, as long as all

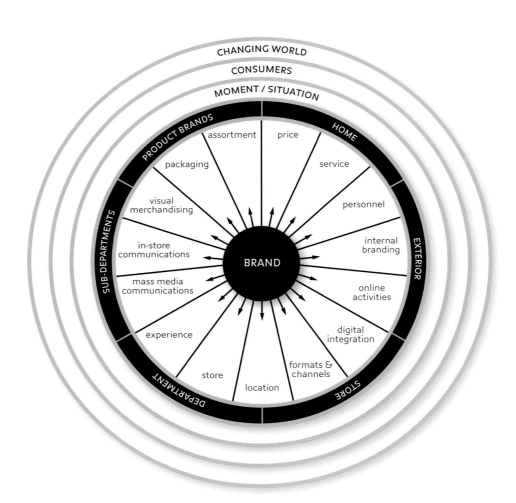

PRICE	SERVICE	PERSONNEL	INTERNAL BRANDING	ONLINE ACTIVITIES
- Maximum/minimum - Price structure - Promotions - Absolute price level (margin mix) - Price-setting methods (volume discounts, credit etc.) - Price image - Relative price level (price recognition)	Pre-sale: - Communications plan Additional services: - e.g Child care After-sales: - Repairs - Made to order (tailloring) - Credit ('money-back returns')	- Training, selection, professional knowledge - Behaviour - Clothing - Tone of voice	- Collective ambition - Values and behavior - Brand identity - Involvement - Organisation culture	- Social media - Online commerce - Web shop - Website - Mobile internet

DIGITAL INTEGRATION	FORMATS & CHANNELS	LOCATION	STORE	EXPERIENCE
- Apps - Internet on shop floor - Webshop - Social media - QR-codes - Self scan - Self service	- Large & mid-sized shops - Future formats - Cross-channel - Webshop - Website - Information - App - Pick-up points (shop & web) - Delivery	- Choices: city centre, periphery, suburb, shopping centre, etc. - Omni-channel - Coverage - Transport - International	- Design - Functional priciples/layout - Routing - Facade/storefront - Lighting, sound, scent	- Expectations versus surprise - Fixed and dynamic elements - Creating conversation value - Attractiveness - Fulfilment - Customer journey

MASS MEDIA COMMUNICATION	IN-STORE COMMUNICATION	VISUAL MERCHANDISING	PACKAGING	ASSORTMENT
- Selecting media channels - Advertising objectives - Sponsoring, ad campaigns, promotions - Themes - Timing - Advertising budget	- Tone & style - Brand image - Logo - Formula level - Product level: products, product groups - Routing and directions - Themes, campaigns	- Point-of-sale materials, displays - Presentation of goods - Store windows	- Branding - Product combinations - Binding factor - Price range - Quality - Distinction	- Collection/accessories - Store brand versus product brands - Product range (breadth, depth) - New products, latest trends - Speed, tempo - Quality - Distribution structure, supply management

■ *Fig. 1 – Explanation of the formula components in the Platform Development Model©.*

55

the elements are dealt with, it can be in any order, at different speeds or even all at once. They have no internal hierarchy as such.

The ambition of the brand forms the outside circumference of the circle. This is the described objective that people are aiming to achieve, the relationship that the brand wishes to engage with its clients, or the established formula concept.

In the formula concept, what has to be realized for each element in a specific store formula has been duly recorded. This might concern a type of store, or in fact several formats and/or channels that together make up the formula. The idea is that all of the parts are entirely filled in. A completed part means that that particular element of the formula has been realized in accordance with the concept.

THE PROCESS IS THE PRODUCT

The inner section of the Platform Development Model© can be used for two purposes. It is a tool for assessing the status quo, on the basis of which the formula can be renewed and further developed, but it also forms the fundamental plan for the development of the retail formula.

The proces is the product, it's a never ending story!

TAKING INVENTORY OF THE STATUS QUO

In order to begin to change, we first have to know where we stand. Here, the Platform Development Model© can be used to produce an overview of the current situation. The various elements can be tested individually and/or in combination with one another against the envisioned brand ambitions. An inventory and analysis per formula element will bring clarity about whether that element needs to be completely changed, partially adapted, or can remain as is.

In embarking on a development process, it is often not entirely clear whether the formula elements have already been fully developed or not. As more knowledge is gained about the direction in which the brand or the store concept is heading, a more accurate and precise inventory will be possible. A variety of phenomena can come to light as a result of the assessment of the various elements.

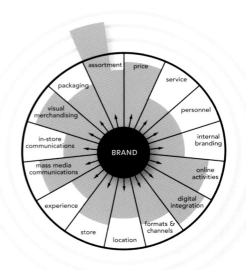

■ *Fig. 2 – Unbalanced assortment.*

I. UNBALANCED ASSORTMENT

As shown in figure 2. One element (in this case the assortment) might be unevenly developed or even overdeveloped. There might be products in the assortment that are ahead of developments in the market, or that do not fit the formula, or there might be products missing that have become essential to that formula.

All retail elements work together in a integrated way.

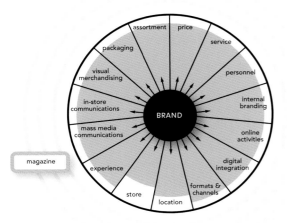

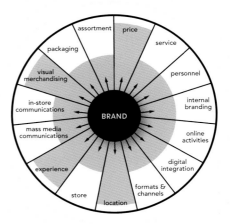

■ *Fig. 3 – Random development of elements.*

■ *Fig. 4 – Underdevelopment.*

II. RANDOM DEVELOPMENT OF ELEMENTS

Figure 3 shows another example. One part of the mass media communications has developed outside the vision of the formula – a magazine, for example. The parameters for this magazine were not determined from the perspective of the needs of the brand, the target group and commercial objectives. Instead, it evolved from an idea of, 'What we think would be a nice magazine'.

III. UNDERDEVELOPMENT

The assessment might produce something like this: the formula includes experience, visual merchandising, location and price, all developed to a comparable degree, but the other parts are underdeveloped in comparison (figure 4). The total picture shows that none of the parts actually benefit the formula concept – the outer periphery. Formula development is therefore required.
Do you want to experience slow and controlled growth, or do you want to capture a large section of the market at a single stroke? In the latter case, the outer periphery will be further away from the core than in the former.

The use of the Platform Development Model© is twofold; it is a tool to assess the status quo of a formula and to develop a new business plan.

It needs to be noted here that the outer circle is not a kind of 'maximum score' that can only be achieved under the most ideal circumstances. Instead, it represents exactly what we want to achieve and are able to achieve at that particular moment. If, for example, the staff do not play an important role (it is rare, but possible), or, as already suggested, they are an element that has already been fully developed, then they will be a part that is already filled in. The outer boundary of the formula concept will have already been reached.

BASIC PLAN FOR FORMULA DEVELOPMENT
During the lifetime of a store formula, there will be some large steps that bring about change, but there will primarily be many small steps. In many cases, a desire for renewal or innovation will evolve when people begin to lose their connection with their changing society. The difficulty is that, for example, a new store design is simply not enough. Adapting one of the elements probably means that the other elements also have to be modified as well.

In addition, the connection with society at large will once again have to be reinforced. For this

reason, one has to take a new look at the brand, the ambition, and the role that the retailer wants to play in the lives of consumers. This enhanced market perspective then serves as input for the Platform Development Model©. For each formula element, people brainstorm about the way in which it can contribute to realizing the ambition and how it can count in being a distinctive factor for the brand. These brainstorming sessions lead to a valuable document, which is full of inspiration, ideas and guidelines for every element in the model, which together form the principles underlying the formula development.

This basic plan can then be linked to a plan of action. Undoubtedly, it may not be possible to execute certain ideas in the short term, and various phases will need to be identified in the formula development. This clearly also depends on the stated ambitions and the situation in which the retail brand finds itself: is it time for a revolutionary change or could the brand and the formula perform better by taking a number of successive evolutionary steps? In any case, in the basic plan and in the phasing, one must ensure that the formula remains a self-contained, evenly balanced circle and that the cohesion remains intact.

The case of a new store can of course be referred to as a major step – it is a revolution. As a result, the whole formula needs to be tackled, as the following examples illustrate. In most cases, this has consequences for all of the elements. In the case of a small step or evolution, or a number of successive evolutionary steps, the outer boundary of the formula concept will shift slowly. The advantage of all these small evolutions is their combined contribution to a fresh, innovative retail formula that stands squarely in the middle of the market.

FORMULA DEVELOPMENT AND PILOT STORE

After design and development, a very important benchmark is the realization of the pilot store. The store is only one of the elements, but it is also the physical or virtual container for the entire formula. All of the formula elements come together here. Ideally, all of the elements are completely developed and realized in the pilot store, so that the effects can be thoroughly studied. Often, however, elements will still be underdeveloped, perhaps, for example, because of lack of time – adapting the assortment is time-consuming – or because the effect of not having done this had been underestimated.

It sometimes happens that once the pilot store is established, development comes to a halt. It is important here to realize that the pilot store is not an end, but a beginning. Once again, assessing the elements and testing the principles of the formula can provide great insight: how do we stand with our new store; have we achieved our ambitions?

People are sometimes inclined to explain possible disappointing results by saying that the pilot store is not a success, when the problem probably lies in an imbalance between the various elements. It is therefore important to view the pilot store as a test case. Then, the exact cause of the disappointment can be identified and resolved.

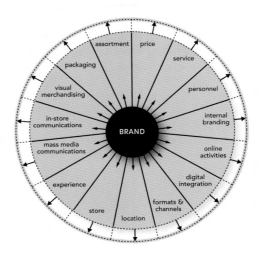

Fig. 5 – Revolutionary formula development.

59

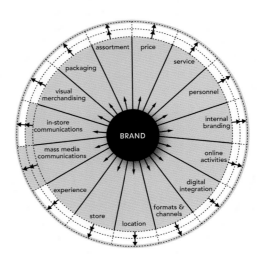

Fig. 6 - Evolutionary formula development.

EVALUATION AND OPTIMIZATION

After the evaluation has been completed, as we again roll out the concept, we may find that it is necessary to take a step back. Elements can in fact disappear, depending on operational or practical problems. The result of this is that the boundaries of the actual formula have to be reined in. In this case, the original formula boundary can sooner be seen as an ideal boundary, towards which people can strive in the years to come.

Figure 7 illustrates this eventuality. The basic principles might be less developed and perhaps even partially changed. The new outer circle now becomes a modified version of the original outer circle, and although the underlying principles can differ, there will certainly be no extreme variations.

Developments of this kind cannot be prevented, but they are not extremely serious. The point is to be aware of them and deal with them with tact. All of the elements have to be put back in place (or to put it more positively, readjusted), so that they all once again come together at the same, new levels. The circle must always be round. Only then does the circle again make sense and function properly.

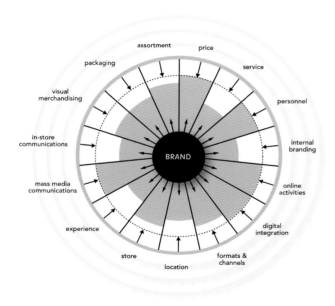

Fig. 7 – Adapting the formula boundary.

Retail is holistic. If one element is changed, every element has to be adapted. The extent to which this happens is determined by the formula concept.

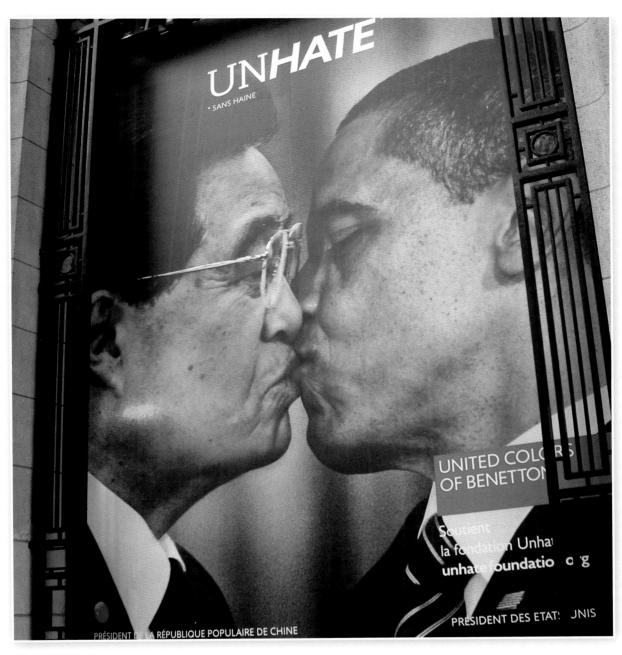

A store enables a brand to show what it
stands for. With its Unhate campaign,
Benetton strives for world peace.
This is their Paris store.

INSIGHT

A STORE FORMULA WILL – OR SHOULD – NEVER STOP DEVELOPING. REMEMBER THAT WE LIVE IN CHANGING SOCIETIES, SOCIETIES THAT ARE ALSO CHANGING FASTER AND FASTER.

One important insight that we want to mention again here is this: changing one element of the formula means that all of the elements will (most probably) change. With one of our clients, we experienced how the stopping power of the formula (the pilot store) had risen sharply, but that the process of conversion failed to meet expectations. Staff were unable to cope with the enormous numbers of visitors in the store. Retraining staff to help them deal with this was crucial. Even though this contingency had been acknowledged and discussed ahead of time, it was only when the store was actually in place that the effect of such a change became visible and convincing.

IN CONCLUSION

IT IS ALWAYS DIFFICULT TO CAPTURE REALITY IN MODELS, BUT MODELS PROVIDE CONSIDERABLE INSIGHT INTO THE SUBSTANCE OF THE MATERIAL AND THE PROBLEMS THAT CAN ARISE.

A holistic approach to the retail formula is vital. In the actual store, all of the elements of the formula come together. In order to achieve successful renewal, it is necessary to chart the cohesion of these elements, beginning with the stated brand concept. When establishing the pilot store, it is important to see it as a challenge: it is a starting point, not an end point.

Practical examples show that an uneven development of elements, or elements that are developed outside the overview of the brand, produce an inconsistent picture, which can have adverse consequences for how consumers experience the formula, and that the formula can never stop developing, whether that happens by way of larger or smaller steps.

In addition to the complexity that the holistic nature of a store formula can bring, in reality, every project can encounter setbacks. Models will not prevent these setbacks, but they certainly can contribute to being able to bend them back into shape, in the positive sense. A setback is also not an end point. Setbacks offer greater incentive to improve on solutions (or, in this case, the respective elements of the formula) and make us better able to assess the possible consequences the next time around.

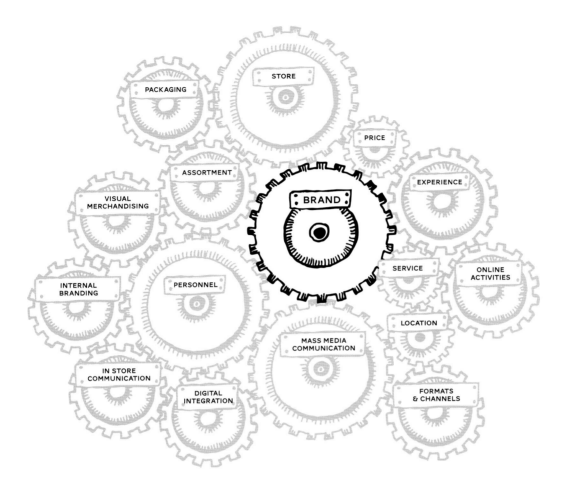

"Retailing 1 to 1 starts with the notion that a store has three distinct aspects: design (meaning the premises), merchandising (whatever you put in them) and operations (whatever employees do). These Big Three, while seemingly separate, are in fact completely intertwined, interrelated and interdependent, meaning that when somebody makes a decision regarding one, a decision has been made about the other two as well."

PACO UNDERHILL

4.
THE EVER CHANGING WORLD

A continuous influence on our lives

ABOUT THE NEED FOR RETAILERS TO ADAPT CONTINUOUSLY, THE MEGA-TRENDS CONVENIENCE AND EXPERIENCE, HOW WE MODIFY OUR EATING AND COOKING HABITS IN RESPONSE TO OUR DAILY ACTIVITIES, THE NEED FOR EASE AND RELEVANCE, EXPERIENCE AS A SUBSTITUTE FOR OR ADDITION TO CONVENIENCE, HOW EXPERIENCE EVOLVES INTO TO MEANING, THE CENTRAL ROLE PLAYED BY THE CUSTOMER, THE ROLE OF DIGITIZATION AND HOW RETAILERS ARE HANGING THE WORLD AND OUR LIVES.

WORLD

'world' comes from the old English 'weorold'
weor = man, old = age
which thus means roughly 'age of man'

Digitization is changing the world. The western world without credit cards is now unimaginable.

THE WORLD IS CONSTANTLY CHANGING, GRADUALLY, BUT SOMETIMES IN LEAPS AND BOUNDS. SOME OF THE WORLD'S CHANGES ARE INFLUENCED BY HUMAN ACTIONS, BUT OUR CHANGING WORLD ALSO CHANGES PEOPLE.

Some changes are so large or abstract, that they have no direct impact on our own lives or one that we only notice much later. Other changes can be felt immediately and give us a different, new perspective on the world or society, which then also affects our behaviour and our needs.

Of course, the changing world and consumer behaviour also have an impact on retail: the one-to-one relationship between the retailer and consumer means that what happens in the world is translated directly to retail. The retailer's right to exist and survive within society is also dependent on his ability to adapt to these changes. The Platform Development tool provides insight into this force field. The consumer is located between the changing world and the retailer and holds a key position. The retailer faces the challenge of keeping the connection with consumers intact (and of course, preferably strengthening it). This connection, in the form of the customer journey, is extremely dynamic, in part because developments in the world appear to be happening at an ever faster pace and in part because the customer journey becomes more varied as new possibilities emerge.

"Companies that do not keep pace with the changing world are doomed."

BEATE VAN DONGEN, PARTNER VODW MARKETING

TRENDS IN THE CHANGING WORLD

DESPITE (OR THANKS TO) THIS DYNAMISM AND VARIETY, THE MANY DIFFERENT TRENDS AND DEVELOPMENTS CAN BE TRACED BACK TO TWO MEGA-TRENDS, THAT HAVE BEEN IN EVIDENCE IN THE WESTERN WORLD FOR SOME YEARS AND ARE EXPECTED TO REMAIN IMPORTANT: CONVENIENCE AND EXPERIENCE.

CONVENIENCE

The first of these mega-trends is convenience: our demand for ease and relevance. We have a lot to do in the course of a day: advancing our careers, being good parents, pursuing an active social life and getting at least an hour of physical exercise as well. That day is never going to be 25 hours long. The enormous increase in the fullness and the speed of everyday western living requires a certain degree of rapid acceptance, adaptation and appreciation. We have to make decisions and do things more quickly. In doing so, we might sometimes wonder which came first – was it the speed of things around us or was it us, hiking up the tempo? The growing flow of information competing for our attention means that it is becoming more difficult and less attractive for us to stop and concentrate for too long on any one thing. Something holds our attention only as long as there is nothing else exciting enough to tempt us away. This process continues to accelerate and is now taken for granted in the western world: if we are not given enough stimulation, we will become bored. This is why retail also needs to change in line with that increased pace. Customer loyalty hardly exists any more and as soon as a better alternative appears, the retailer has lost the customer.

Relevance and convenience are the decisive factors in this. Consumers need to be able to recognize the personal advantage these offer and this needs to be of benefit both in buying and using the product. What is relevant varies from person to person, depending on their circumstances or their mood. A family has different needs and a different lifestyle than a retired couple, or someone who lives alone. For example, product combinations, product suggestions and advance selections in the store help make the decision to purchase easier, and single or two-person portions make the products relevant for the customer. In addition, the development of different store formats and channels enables retailers to give consumers the right products in the right places.

The dynamism that exist between retail and the changing world can be nicely illustrated with the help of the example of changing eating habits in western societies. Here too, convenience is a major factor. Influenced by changes in the make-up of the typical household and increased time pressure, we have had to reduce the time we spend in our kitchens. We now spend only about twenty minutes preparing a meal. The formula of the Dutch supermarket chain, Albert Heijn, is a good example of a retail store offering a clear reflection of these developments.

At the store level, Albert Heijn stands out in the faster world of its customers by serving them in various ways. At the Albert Heijn ToGo convenience concept stores, at train stations and on high streets, shoppers can quickly purchase a snack, sandwich or coffee to consume on the move. But they can also buy whatever they might have forgotten when they were doing their general grocery shopping, so that they do not have to go out again to purchase it. Albert Heijn XL is at the other end of the spectrum, the largest of the store variations, where the focus is on one-stop shopping, and in addition to a wide assortment of food products, non-food products are also available. The XL stores are often farther away from city centres and have ample parking facilities, so the inconvenience of heavy shopping bags is minimized for the customer. Albert Heijn also offers the possibility of ordering groceries online and having them delivered to your home. This way, consumers are saved the time and trouble of doing their weekly shopping themselves. If you simply walk into the supermarket, the 'Appie' mobile app makes it all easier, with a recipe search, an overview of products on offer and even a feature for compiling your shopping list. All of the products on that list will then be arranged according to their location as you follow the routing through the store.

At product level, the approach also focuses on the customer. In its assortment, Albert Heijn offers different packaging sizes to suit the different needs of its customers. A range of meal suggestions are provided, and in addition to the regular assortment, there are also quick and healthy ready meals, steamed meals, pre-cut vegetables, pre-cooked pasta or rice and much more. Everything is designed to make it easier for customers to decide what they could have for their evening meal.

■ Above: a customer at Marks & Spencer uses a magnifying glass to read the package contents. Retailers will need to respond to the ageing population.

Left: the speed of our daily lives means that people have a greater need for convenience. Retailers respond by offering convenience concepts. The Dutch supermarket chain Albert Heijn has developed AH toGo.

EXPERIENCE

There is a second mega-trend that runs parallel with convenience, and that is experience. To stay for a moment with the example of our changing eating habits: TV chefs such as Jamie Oliver and Gordon Ramsey and a variety of cooking programmes on television show us what cooking with passion is all about. Here, the art of cooking is made accessible, and it has become very popular. We invite friends or family to our homes for a meal, and we can try to impress them with our culinary skills. Being able to tell them where a particular dish comes from, or from which famous chef, makes it even more special.

The ways that we cook today also reflect broader trends at play in society at large. In this sense, it all goes hand-in-hand with our focus on self-actualization and personal enrichment. Globalization has brought us in contact with other cultures and ingredients, so that we are perfectly happy cooking with a wok and we can find exotic spices, such as curry and coconut milk, in our local supermarket. According to philosopher Stine Jensen, television cooking programmes have changed: in the 1990s, the emphasis was on losing weight, while today's focus is all about good health.

Kathleen Collins states that the popularity of cooking is a result of our desire for nostalgia and honest craftsmanship. Collins is the author of the book, Watching What We Eat: The Evolution of Television Cooking Shows. Because we spend so much time on mental activities or working with the computer, we are searching for a counterweight. In this sense, cooking is the embodiment of physical labour with a concrete and honest result. This need for physical labour also explains the popularity of gardening and DIY. Cooking is just like building something. It is honest, authentic and sexy, and perhaps most importantly it is something everybody can do. All we have to do is have the desire and the focus.

The experience trend offers a necessary alternative to convenience, because if something cannot be done quickly, or if you do not want it to be fast, then it should be a valuable and special way of spending your time. In the book, The Experience Economy, authors Pine and Gilmore describe the power of transforming a generic process into a real experience. It is the intangible, added value that means that consumers go out of their way for it or are willing to pay more for it. Nonetheless, relevance is essential here too, in order to continue to offer consumers that added value. Each time, that shopper has to be offered an innovative, surprising and understandable experience. This does not mean that it should be some kind of Disneyland experience: the experience can be very subtle and personal, the story of the origins of a particular tea or coffee, for example. That is something you want to tell your friends about over dinner. It makes the coffee or tea special, and it says something about you, about your taste for quality and for exceptional things. The same is true of stores. There too, it is important to offer shoppers a unique experience every time they come into the store. Something that transcends the need for convenience and means that the customer will keep coming back. Here, we can build on the ideas of Pine and Gilmore, who argue that the world has changed from commodity to service, and from service to experience. It is now time to evolve from experience to meaningfulness.

In retail there are two mega-trends: convenience and experience.

■ As a counter-movement to the fast pace of life, we are increasingly looking for crafts-manship and quality. This explains the popularity of London's Borough Market.

A good experience is a valuable and special way of passing time. Eataly brings Italian food close to you. Originally Italian, it's now also located in New York.

IT IS TIME TO EVOLVE FROM EXPERIENCE TO MEANINGFULNESS

CONVENIENCE AND EXPERIENCE

In our world, which is moving ever faster, we also need to be able to access everything more quickly. This is why offering convenience is essential. Or if that's not possible, experience makes a good substitute. But the next step involves finding a combination of convenience and experience. This combination can be integrated or the two can be offered alongside each other. This depends on such factors as the sector, the customers and how the product is used. This combination of trends can only be properly achieved by putting the customer first and offering a solution that perfectly matches his desires and mindset.

For example, in a garden centre, this combination of both experience and convenience can be achieved as follows. Sometimes people are simply in the mood to visit a garden centre. Then it takes on the form of a pleasant excursion: finding inspiration for one's own garden, browsing through the wide assortment of plants and checking out the latest trends and garden furniture. People may then stop off for coffee and cake in the restaurant. In this case, the focus is on experience. However, if someone is planning to spend Saturday tidying up the garden, they will need a quicker and more targeted trip to the garden centre. In this case, helpful solutions include a fast lane through the garden centre, offering an appropriate assortment featuring seasonal plants, tips on how to plant, potting compost and a selection of garden tools, or the opportunity to order online and collect the items in the store or even have them delivered.

In order to be able to offer a distinctive proposition, more experience will also need to be added to convenience concepts. A good example is the Vapiano restaurant chain, founded by former McDonald's staff in Germany. The knowledge they had acquired at the fast food chain helped them to realize that fast food need not necessarily be fast and unhealthy. Vapiano positions itself as a fast casual restaurant, based on the principles of self-service, tasty food and a pleasant atmosphere. When you arrive, you are given a card on which to record your order, which you do not have to pay for until you leave via the checkout. You order the food you want yourself in an open kitchen. The Italian dishes are simple and are freshly prepared while you wait and watch. The experience is also like that of a restaurant, where you can spend the whole evening or simply have a quick meal. Tables at different levels, a bar and benches allow guests to choose what best suits them at that time.

DIGITIZING THE WORLD

THE ABILITY TO OFFER A COMBINATION OF CONVENIENCE AND EXPERIENCE IS BEING ACCELERATED BY THE NUMEROUS POSSIBILITIES OFFERED BY DIGITIZATION AND BY ITS RAPID ACCEPTANCE BY CONSUMERS.

Retail directly translates developments taking place in society into a form that is useful for that society. The Fitch design agency's 1990 book, 'Fitch on Retail Design', about mail-order shopping, call centres and television shopping channels – channels that have increasingly lost their relevance in the modern day – did not at the time have anything to say about the internet, smartphones or social media. Now, just over two decades later, the internet has become an inextricable part of the omni-channel strategies used by increasing numbers of retailers. It is almost impossible to believe that the internet has existed for only slightly more than 5000 days. In that short time, a great deal has changed, and new possibilities are being developed at tremendous speed.

Because of digitization, consumers have become accustomed to the transparency of what is on offer and the fact that it is available 24 hours a day, seven days a week. People can access the internet on their laptop, smartphone and tablet and cannot only find literally everything they need, but they also have a huge load of information thrown at them. The phenomenon has been called 'infobesity': people have become addicted to information, impulses, visual stimuli. People have coped amazingly well with this: they know how to absorb all the information they need quickly, although they may skim read it rather than in-depth. Nevertheless, they know exactly how to find what interests them and often even use several channels simultaneously. No doubt you will recognize

the scenario: watching TV with a laptop or tablet on your lap, with a smartphone within reach. The TV has become little more than background music, but we still leave it switched on. With half an eye on a film or TV programme, we Google for all sorts of things, check our e-mail, use Facebook and Whatsapp to communicate with friends.

Retail is becoming more personal and interactive; so even more one-to-one.

CONSEQUENCES FOR RETAILERS

Developments on the internet, in digital communication and multimedia usage are making our world increasingly interactive and the number of channels we can use is steadily increasing. Ebay, where we can trade, the long tail we use to search for the product or service we want, often on the other side of the planet. Shopping together with friends on social media and communicating with retailers and other shoppers, on blogs, interactive websites and so on. For retailers, it has become necessary to engage in interaction with the customer, to enter into contact with him or her, explore what the customer wants and negotiate a way forward. With that knowledge, suppliers and retailers are better able to offer custom-made products and solutions for individual customers. Once you have bought something on a website or logged onto it, you will be personally addressed the next time you visit, which never happens at the supermarket you visit four times a week. This means retail is becoming more personal and more interactive. In his book, Het nieuwe winkelen

(The New Way of Shopping), Cor Molenaar calls this shift the transition from the supply paradox to the demand paradox: through interaction, the retailer can gain a better understanding of what the customer wants and put together a customized assortment instead of the client purchasing what the retailer happens to have available. The demand paradox not only applies to the assortment, but also the way in which it is offered: a retailer should not start a webshop alongside its physical store or launch a Facebook page or blog simply because that is the appropriate thing to do and the competition is also doing it. Instead, the retailer needs to explore how to approach consumers in an appropriate way and place. This kind of consumer-centric retail increasingly involves several channels that work together and complement each other: pure players are becoming mixed players.

In the customer journey, the consumer uses several channels and resources, alternately and simultaneously, and in order to maintain the connection throughout this customer journey, the retailer also needs to use multiple channels. This means that the retailer becomes more focused on the customer and more one-to-one. In fact, it means that the customer and retailer are placed alongside each other and the relationship becomes more equal. This raises an interesting question: can the customer, who is on familiar terms with the supplier, who helps decide what is on the shelves, what services are offered and what prices are charged and who helps determine the right pricing, still be called king and behave accordingly? Because he can now express opinions, engage in discussions with other customers and the supplier. He can make suggestions, impose demands, purchase or boycott. You might even say that the customer, or buyer, now has much of the power. If you engage in a lot of interaction, take part in decision-making, behave in a friendly way, etc., it is no longer appropriate to continue behaving as a king or indeed to expect to be treated like one. You actually become more a partner in crime and the age-old hierarchy can no longer be sustained.

Smartphones play an increasingly important role in our lives and add a new dynamic to the way we shop. These consumers are outside Saks Fifth Avenue in New York City.

"Don't find customers for your products, find products for your customers."

SETH GODIN

RETAILERS CHANGE
THE WORLD

SO FAR, WE HAVE CONCENTRATED ON CHANGES IN THE WORLD AND THE IMPORTANCE FOR RETAILERS OF ANTICIPATING THESE CHANGES, BUT THINGS CAN ALSO WORK THE OTHER WAY AROUND. RETAIL CAN CHANGE THE WORLD.

Companies such as Apple and IKEA have transformed retail to such an extent that we have changed the way we shop and the way we live. This is a result of the innovative character of the organizations. They saw the changes in society, followed technological developments, predicted the opportunities and had just the right timing.

Although at the time, no one would have been able to predict that – or how – listening to music and purchasing music could change so radically, today, nothing in music is the way it used to be. Nowadays large groups of people only listen to and download digitally. This has opened up entirely new possibilities for consumers to enjoy music. The fall in sales of CDs threatens the very existence of music stores. A few music lovers still go to the shops, just for the experience. They see this as a moment of luxury, a way of pampering themselves. The relationship with the staff in the store and personal advice are often important reasons for going. Clearly, consumers saw the advantages offered by digital music, signed up to this new, better or more efficient way of satisfying their needs, and moved over to the new media en masse. The way they use music has changed from ownership to access. The advantage for the consumer is that this new form is both easier and cheaper. Apple jumped into the mix at a very early stage and made its contribution with the launch of the iPod and iTunes. In fact, Apple has totally transformed and expanded the way we use media. In 2011, Steve Jobs even won a Grammy for

his contribution to the music industry. What was originally a computer company is now one of the largest media companies in the world.

Alongside the continued development of media, design and ease of use have also made their mark. Ease of use, achieved through design, means that Apple has turned its customers into true fans, devotees who stand in long lines at Apple stores every time a new product is launched. In product development, Apple puts the user first. Existing features are optimized so that ease of use has priority and is always being improved. By also placing greater emphasis on product design, the brand has two important cornerstones that give it enormous added value. The popularity of a brand such as Apple has brought user-centric design to large numbers of people. It is easy to become accustomed to this combination of attractive design and ease of use and it quickly becomes the new standard. Products like this are fun and practical: they are gadgets with a purpose. In their processes of innovation, companies will increasingly focus on design, because this is no longer simply the preserve of a select few.

"The brands that will have the greatest impact on all our lives are those that see themselves not as citadels that need defending, but as causes that need joining."

NICK KEPPEL-PALMER, WOLFF OLINS

IKEA has also made a major contribution to this development by making home and living products accessible and affordable for a large group of people. When this retailer appeared in our cities and towns, we changed the way we furnished and decorated our homes. Traditional furniture stores sold almost exclusively expensive products, so-called capital goods, that were often hand-crafted and, because of their price and quality, would last

People are invited to use all the Apple products in the Apple store at Grand Central Station in New York City.

Truly innovative retailers can change the way we live.

almost a lifetime. The delivery times reflected this. IKEA broke with this tradition by adopting an entirely different approach to the marketplace. They began with industrially mass-produced, very affordable products that customers could pick up themselves from the stores and had to assemble at home. This offered us new ideas for styling that changed our tastes and made it possible to furnish and decorate our homes relatively cheaply. It even enabled us to restyle our homes from time to time by incorporating changes to the decor. When young people left their family homes, they were no longer compelled to take only the hand-me-downs from home that reflected the tastes of their parents, but could express their own identities by designing their home interiors themselves. The rise of the social society in Sweden and the rest of Europe meant that young people were more independent of their parents and no longer had to live at home until they had permanent employment and were married. As a result, demand for affordable furniture and individual styles grew. As the first store to offer low-cost furniture, IKEA facilitated this process of growing independence, making it easier for young people to leave their parental homes sooner. The success of the innovative IKEA business plan is thanks to its adaptability or relevance in the context of that particular period. The development of their business concept has its origins back in 1956 and was based on minimal service and maximum customer participation, in stark contrast to accepted retail standards of the day. Customers had to collect the products in the stores, take them home and assemble them themselves. The furniture was also packed in efficient, flat boxes. All of this brought down costs, keeping prices low for customers. Twenty years earlier, that same business idea would probably have failed, because it would not have reflected society at the time and would therefore not have been the obvious choice for contemporary consumers. For the same reason, the IKEA formula has also transformed itself over time. It has to remain relevant and continue to reflect the spirit of the times. Clearly, IKEA focuses strongly on the needs of consumers. With the rise of the service society, IKEA became more service-oriented, and it continues to develop additional services available. Their kitchen departments increasingly consist of computer terminals where people can design their own kitchens and configure them to their taste. If necessary, they can ask IKEA staff for help. In addition to this form of mass customization, there are also various practical aftersales services integrated into the company, including a transport service, assembly service and even a shop assistant who collects your purchases in the warehouse while you enjoy a hot dog. As a customer, you can control the cost and the ease of shopping at IKEA, to suit your individual needs. IKEA offers solutions that are targeted to different types of customers and their mindsets. It is up to the customer to decide what he wants.

■ Above: Retailers must adapt to the changing world or forfeit their right to exist. This electronics store is forced to close its doors after 22 years of business.

■ IKEA has changed the world and given people the self-confidence to create their own style. In this mass media campaign, 'everyone is a designer'.

TIMING AND VISION

HOW DO WE STRIKE A BALANCE BETWEEN ACCEPTING THE CHANGING WORLD AND CHANGING IT OURSELVES?

The answer lies in the right timing and a well-founded vision. To have timing and vision, we need intensive knowledge of the changes that are happening and the impact they have. Then we must act accordingly. These insights have to be translated into the disciplines of retail. Formula management is very important here, because to be able to change quickly, we need effective control and direction in order to make the holistic formula into an actual, functioning whole. In many cases, the most successful, influential retailers are organizations that have vertical integration, because they have all the aspects of business management in hand, from purchasing raw materials to the production process, to the visual merchandising in the stores, from formula development to organization management. In such organizations as these, adaptations can be made relatively quickly and in a structured manner, resulting in a shopping experience that remains relevant and authentic.
A vertically-integrated organization also sells only its own labels, instead of different product brands. This makes these retail brands and their assortments unique and unlike any others. IKEA, Apple, H&M and Zara are all examples of vertically-integrated retail organizations.

To be able to change the world, it is necessary to stay a step ahead. Innovation is important. With a clear vision of what is happening and what is likely to happen, new things are created, things that we had no knowledge of beforehand and could not previously have imagined. Here, a solid dose of entrepreneurship is required to breathe life into the dream we are creating, and to keep that dream alive.

The model below shows what resources are required in order to achieve growth and change and what happens if these resources are only available in insufficient number or not at all. But they not only need to be there, they also need to work together: and they need to be able to do so holistically.

To achieve growth and change, a company has to work with its strengths.

The vision of society and the market, and the role that the company wishes to play within them, is then recorded in the strategy. On the one hand, this vision must match what is going on outside the company as well as the structure and culture of the organization in order to enable it to capitalize on its strengths: this ensures that people are motivated and can work in an organized way. Ultimately, human capacity and resources are required in order to actually achieve the strategy. Working towards a concrete final result and experiencing progress on the way there ensures that people remain motivated in order to achieve the necessary growth and change. In this, a deadline is a key motivating factor that arises from the strategy: it is this that determines the right timing.

	STRUCTURE processes and organisation	CULTURE leadership and basic values	PEOPLE competencies and skills	RECOURCES ICT, money and facilities	RESULTS products and effects	= CONFUSION no coherence and vision
STRATEGY scenarios and architecture		CULTURE leadership and basic values	PEOPLE competencies and skills	RECOURCES ICT, money and facilities	RESULTS products and effects	= CHAOS no direction and control
STRATEGY scenarios and architecture	STRUCTURE processes and organisation		PEOPLE competencies and skills	RECOURCES ICT, money and facilities	RESULTS products and effects	= RESISTANCE no bonding
STRATEGY scenarios and architecture	STRUCTURE processes and organisation	CULTURE leadership and basic values		RECOURCES ICT, money and facilities	RESULTS products and effects	= ANXIETY no skills
STRATEGY scenarios and architecture	STRUCTURE processes and organisation	CULTURE leadership and basic values	PEOPLE competencies and skills		RESULTS products and effects	= FRUSTRATION no facilities
STRATEGY scenarios and architecture	STRUCTURE processes and organisation	CULTURE leadership and basic values	PEOPLE competencies and skills	RECOURCES ICT, money and facilities		= FUTILITY no added value
STRATEGY scenarios and architecture	STRUCTURE processes and organisation	CULTURE leadership and basic values	PEOPLE competencies and skills	RECOURCES ICT, money and facilities	RESULTS products and effects	= GROWTH AND CHANGE

The essential ingredients for growth and change. A model by M.A. Nieuwenhuis in The Art of Management.

5.
THE CONSUMER

The pivotal role in retail

ABOUT THE DYNAMICS OF CONSUMER BEHAVIOUR, MASLOW'S THEORY
OF HUMAN MOTIVATIONS, THE ROLE OF BRANDS IN SELF-BRANDING, PEER
GROUP PRESSURE, TARGET GROUP SEGMENTATION, THE DIFFERENCES
BETWEEN MEN AND WOMEN, THE INFLUENCES OF PARTICULAR MOMENTS
AND SITUATIONS AND THE VARIOUS REASONS FOR SHOPPING.

80%

The 'dutch consumers' are women. She decides in 80% of the purchasing decisions.

■ *Flower market at Plaza Duomo in Milan,
viewed from above.*

THIS IS THE MARKET – LITERALLY AND FIGURATIVELY. THESE ARE CONSUMERS, AND IN FACT EVERYTHING THAT WE KNOW ABOUT THOSE CONSUMERS. INDEED, WE CAN ONLY OBSERVE THEM AS WE SEE THEM IN THIS PHOTOGRAPH: LOOKING DOWN, FROM A DISTANCE.

You might wonder why these people are there. Have they come for the flower market, or for the inviting cafes that no doubt surround the market square? Are they there because of the cathedral – the Milan Duomo looks out over this city square – or are they just crossing the square on their way home? We cannot tell just by looking at them.

Would they come here especially to buy flowers or plants, and if so, why? This literally and figuratively has to do with how the flower vendor has positioned himself: literally because he is at this particular location and figuratively because he has established himself as an open-air market seller and not, for example, in a flower shop on a shopping street. What this is about is making a

decision, choosing a certain identity and the associated image it projects. The plants themselves make no difference. People can buy them anywhere and they are always more or less the same. There will not be any great difference in quality or price at this location. Indeed, if one seller is particularly successful with a plant of a certain quality and price here today, next week, the other sellers will all be sure to have a similar product for sale. No, here, customers are buying because of the location, the ambiance and the atmosphere that surrounds them.

So why are they buying from one seller and not the other? It sometimes seems like coincidence, and there are times when it is coincidence, but in most cases, people choose a combination of personality traits and presentation. They select an entrepreneur who clearly shows them who he is, usually unobtrusively and without actually being aware of doing it. This is a kind of clarity created by the decisions the entrepreneur makes, by being the person he is, with his feeling for the marketplace and for the products on offer.

HUMAN MOTIVATIONS AND CONSUMER BEHAVIOUR

At an open air market, it is still relatively simple for customers to compare different sellers, simply by walking past, looking at the wares, at how the sellers present themselves and, not unimportantly, at who else is buying. People are attracted to other, like-minded people.

Of course, marketing and consumer research can reveal greater detail about the considerations and choices consumers make. Different target groups can be identified and, with the help of customer loyalty cards, their purchasing habits can be analysed. Ultimately, however, shopping behaviour is so complex, dynamic and dependent on so many factors and motivations that it cannot simply be captured in models or statistics.

TO GAIN A PICTURE OF THE BEHAVIOUR AND THE MOTIVATIONS OF CONSUMERS, WE INSTEAD TURN TO OUR DEEP-SEATED ROOTS.

For as far back as anyone can remember, shopping has been a social affair, and it is the nature of human beings to collect things that might not be relevant because of their specific function as such, but that express the identity, rank and status of their owners. This has always been the case and will always continue to be so. Whether it is a symbol of the tribe to which we belong, a medal worn on a uniform, a facial cream or a pair of sports shoes, it all says something about who we are and is consciously selected in this context. In other words, making a purchase is a means of expression for an individual and a reinforcement of that individual's social standing. The choice might

86

■ *Maslow's pyramid as it is now.*

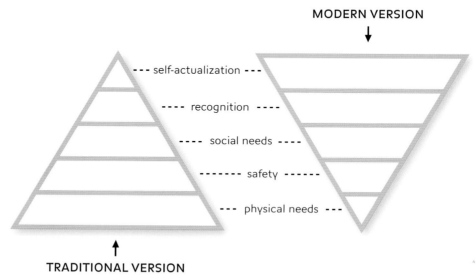

be determined by birth, or by the environment in which one grows up, or by pressure from one's peers. We are social creatures. It is important to show which group we belong to and what our place is in that group.

We spend most of our time trying to achieve acknowledgement and self-actualisation.

Being able to demonstrate our position in society is a consequence of changes in the way our societies are organized and, on the other hand, our increasing prosperity and improved living conditions. A visual illustration of this human development can be seen in Abraham Maslow's 'Hierarchy of Needs' (1954). Maslow's theory is about human motivations. It remains popular because of its relevance for our daily lives and the fact that it can be practically applied to so many situations. There has been significant criticism of this model, but it is still very useful in explaining some aspects of consumer behaviour.

The essence of Maslow's theory is that our fundamental needs, which are at the bottom of the first pyramid, first have to be satisfied, before the subsequent layer of needs becomes relevant. As long as people do not have enough to eat and drink, they will not be able to concern themselves with safety and security. But as soon as those physical needs are satisfied, people will put great effort into their focus on security. Not having that security will give them a very unsatisfied feeling.

In the same way, our search for more will always exist, until we reach the top of the pyramid. The top of the pyramid is self-actualization, where we are satisfied and accept things as they are and therefore no longer strive for more.

In the western world, it can be said that in general, the needs expressed in the first three layers of the pyramid have been satisfied. In principle, everyone has access to enough food. We live in a welfare state in which our security is guarded by higher authorities. Even though our societies are individualistic in character, most people have the necessary family members and friends around them for support. For this reason, in our everyday lives, we are primarily focused on the top layers of the pyramid. We are in search of recognition and respect and, in some cases, even self-actualization. Because we devote most of our time to this, we can say that we have turned the Maslow pyramid upside down: we spend the least energy in satisfying our physical needs and most of our energy in gaining the respect of others or achieving self-actualization.

RECOGNITION

Most people in western societies now find themselves in the fourth layer of Maslow's pyramid. This tells us a lot about where we stand in life. We want to enjoy 'our own lives'. This certainly influences our attitudes and behaviour towards our surroundings, how we act as consumers and the factors that matter to us. In this layer of the pyramid, is the ego that first needs to be satisfied, before we consider other people. The question that we are always – consciously or otherwise – asking is, 'What's in it for me?' On a Sunday afternoon, do we visit our great aunt on her birthday or go for a drink with our friends? Or, how do I feel when I am in this store; what does it say about me that I can be found in this particular brand environment, and what will those around me think about that? Status plays an exceptionally important role for people who have achieved this layer of the Maslow's pyramid, even as they continue to strive for even higher status. In order to make the desired status available to a larger public, we see luxury clothing brands, such as Louis Vuitton, developing a variety of associated product lines including small bags, iPhone and iPad cases and perfumes. For a relatively affordable price, people can show those around them the kinds of luxuries they can allow themselves.

The migration from the third to the fourth layer in Maslow's pyramid did not happen all by itself. It came hand in hand with a meritocratic society, higher living standards, globalization, secularization and the emancipation of women. The meritocracy began in the United States, where the lack of a long historical tradition brought with it a lack of established order and aristocracy, as well as the idea of 'the American dream', in which everyone, from newspaper boy to millionaire, had the same opportunities.

> *"Our expectations continue to grow unabated, nurtured by the ideology of the meritocracy"*
>
> **ALAIN DE BOTTON, 'STATUS ANXIETY'**

In his book, Status Anxiety, Alain de Botton describes how, influenced by the ideology of meritocracy, the endless pursuit for more will always exist. This ideology is, to a greater or lesser degree, found widely throughout the entire western world and is also beginning to emerge in Asia. The result is that, in theory, everyone has the chance to take his life into his own hands and become a success, and that everyone therefore expects this of themselves. According to de Botton, this also means that if you do not succeed, you are a failure, a 'loser'. Such concepts as 'a loser', 'a nobody', and phrases such as 'get a life' are therefore the fruits of this kind of society. These expectations, which continue to grow, are illustrated by the person who earns his first €100,000, and looks around with great satisfaction, then quickly observes that there are suddenly people with €100,000 or more all around. The seeds of dissatisfaction have been sown, together with the ambition to strive for more.

The prosperity we enjoy today has removed certain anxieties and concerns, reducing our need to ensure our security, leaving us free to discover and experiment more and develop ourselves.

Where people used to see themselves as part of a family, a church community and so on, and functioned – largely – within that group, with shared standards and values and a common identity that to a significant degree determined who they were, today, it is much more up to us to determine who we are. We are expected to take care of ourselves, keep ourselves informed and have an opinion, forming our own standards and values and creating and expressing our own personal identity. The role of the family has much less impact in determining what the course of our lives will be. With globalization, we experience an ever-increasing assortment of cultural convictions and traditions and a wider range of ideas about moral obligations with which we can identify. The great motto of our contemporary society is, 'Improve yourself!' Individual development, in terms of knowledge, career and spirituality is the great goal. Relationships and interrelationships have changed. In personal relations, who the individual person is and their independence are important factors. It is in this context that we also see that people are remaining single for longer or becoming single more often.

Individualization also means that society has become increasingly anonymous. Nonetheless, we still need to provide ourselves with a place within that larger whole. This is because we are group animals by nature. We want to be appreciated and receive acknowledgement for who we are from the people whom we in turn appreciate. This also distinguishes different groups of people. It makes them more segmented: we feel at home with one group, but not with another. It used to be enough to be Catholic, Protestant or communist, but this no longer applies today. As a result, more and more people are inclined towards 'self-branding', expressing a self-created image of themselves. One relatively new form of self-branding is taking place via social media. In this process, social media serve both as a facilitator and as a catalyst, making it possible – and therefore virtually essential – for people 'to belong', to be part of something, to stay informed of what is happening in the world and be able to participate in daily conversations. Here, people can also take advantage of the opportunity to base that self-image more on who they would like to be or who they would like others to think they are.
This makes customer segmentation all the more complex.

> *"Time and again, as someone takes a step up the career ladder, they purchase different brands, using this to make a statement to their environment: 'I have arrived.'"*

**ROLAND VAN KRALINGEN,
'SUPERBRANDS'**

Allowing ourselves to be associated with certain brands is one form of self-branding that we have been familiar with for several years. Based on the possessions with which we surround ourselves, we form and express our identities. Brands are frequently used to express status. People can use them to reveal what they have accomplished, what they consider important; that they, for example, have exclusive taste or enjoy a certain kind of music. Roland van Kralingen explains in his book, Superbrands: "Time and again, as someone takes a step up the career ladder, they purchase different brands, using this to make a statement to their environment: 'I have arrived.'" The shirt with the Polo pony logo, the SUV parked in front of the house – they are all status symbols that help make us part of our peer group. Brands consequently play an increasingly greater role in retail. Aside from what we buy, in self-branding it also matters where we buy. We can then show this to our fellow consumers through the shopping bags we carry.

SELF-ACTUALIZATION

It could be argued that in western societies today, there is a tendency towards a move from the fourth to the fifth level of the pyramid. When someone has reached the fifth layer, the top of the pyramid, they have achieved a state of satisfaction. At this stage, brands can still function as a means of identification, but material status symbols as an expression of financial success now have very little importance. In self-actualization, inner balance and meaning dominate. This tendency can be recognized in the growing demand for responsible products, such as organically grown foods, mindfulness products, green energy, fairtrade products, electric-powered transport and cradle-to-cradle building and manufacturing concepts. In recent years, there also appears to be a slow but consistent growth in the numbers of people who are prepared to pay more for sustainable products. They are driven by a desire to make responsible choices, without gaining any direct personal advantage.

Changes in society that may have helped drive this tendency include the 2008 credit crisis, increasing awareness of environmental issues and religious debates about inherent standards and values, as well as simple consumption fatigue. We have been seen that having everything we want does not make us happier. We now know that everything is possible, that new technological developments are happening so quickly that we cannot even keep up with them. This has reduced the pressure once felt. Many people have become more critical about their purchases and are looking for brands that satisfy a need to find real meaning. Philip Kotler describes this tendency at length in Marketing 3.0. Although this might also be related to status and could just be a temporary trend ('Look how hip I am; I buy green!'), it is

nonetheless a trend that is not specifically an expression of financial success. It is therefore very different in character than behaviour generated by the status anxiety described by de Botton. Status has now taken on an entirely different meaning or value. If we accept this prediction as fact, we could conclude that brands must become more meaningful, representing company missions that relate more to the desires and needs of self-actualized individuals and less to pretentious lifestyles. In this case, the way brands are developed and communicated would need to change in order to retain that crucial contact with consumers.

◼ *One expression of self-actualization is the growing demand for responsible products, as seen at London's Borough Market.*

INTRODUCING:
THE AVERAGE CONSUMER

TO DEVELOP A CLEAR IDEA OF CONSUMER BEHAVIOUR AND MOTIVATIONS, IT IS IMPORTANT TO KNOW THE 'AVERAGE' CONSUMERS, THE MASSES WHO FORM THE MAJOR PORTION OF THE MARKET. THIS OFFERS INSIGHT INTO HOW ANY ENVISIONED TARGET GROUP RELATES TO THE MIDDLE SEGMENT OF THE MARKET.

For example, they are the trendsetters, the 'early adopters', or the status-sensitive. They are actively engaged with striving to attain Maslow's objectives and want to be at the vanguard. Others may be more inclined to be followers. If the objective is to speak to the masses, then it is certainly this group that must be kept in mind.

The photograph is a good illustration of average Dutch consumers and was taken during the Libelle Summer Week. Libelle, one of the Netherlands' largest and oldest magazines, organizes this annual event, which is attended by masses of women who come for a day out with other female friends or family. They attend fashion shows, lectures, makeovers and workshops, and there are also countless opportunities for retail therapy. The success of the Libelle Summer Week is because the organizers have been able to offer activities and entertainment that are precisely geared to appeal to women who are active, practically inclined, and who enjoy each other's company. Dutch women, like those illustrated in the photograph, are the backbone of Dutch society. They determine what happens in the Netherlands and they decide what people purchase. Indeed, women make 80% of all purchasing decisions. They have single earning power but double the spending power, because they spend not only their own salaries but also those of their partners. It is therefore very important to understand that

this is the Dutch consumer, the target group that we are concerned with, at least if the retailer's objective is to appeal to the middle segment.

The photograph shows Dutch men, on holiday. That means that they will no doubt be in a different state of mind: relaxed and not in a hurry. One thing, however, has not changed. They are standing outside a store, waiting (probably for their female counterparts or family members). In general, men do not like shopping. This is something that is determined by nature. Men are hunters. They are goal-oriented and focused on finding the target. In retail terms, this means they are destination shoppers. Women, in contrast, want to seek. When men were out hunting, women were searching for nuts, berries and edible plants, in case their men came home empty-handed.

This gives us an important insight into how we can make consumers our customers, and how we can best serve them. We must also not forget the undoubtedly less obvious moments, such as when a man sits in a store, waiting for his wife or daughter, bored. This must be the perfect moment to introduce him to a brand or product that would interest him.

Retailers are inclined not to want to exclude anyone, so they naturally want to see every consumer as a potential customer. Nonetheless, retailers will ultimately have to target their activities at a single, or at just a few segments of the market. Specialization and making choices is necessary, because as a retailer, you otherwise become too generic: if the target group is too broad, you become unclear, and no one is attracted to you. Seen from the perspective of the consumers, they want to have the feeling that they are being approached and treated as unique individuals. In order for

Men want to find; women want to search.

retailers to be able to define their target clearly, it is essential to have knowledge of the lives and the needs of consumers, both consumers generally and those in the specific target group. Only with this insight can a retailer anticipate the needs of customers and be attractive to them. Even if a single man purchases socks for his children at Zeeman and a tie for himself at De Bijenkorf, he has a completely different attitude in each of these two different stores. He then makes his decisions for different reasons, and he will have to be approached differently in each situation.

Qualitative researcher and CEO of Ferro Explore, Jochum Stienstra, has described the developments taking place in market segmentation. Initially, people were arranged according to sex, age, level of education and family status. This data gave enough insight into target groups for companies to position themselves in the mar-

Women are our most important consumers. They determine 80% of purchases. They also combine single earning power with double spending power.

Above: Dutch women are active, practical and love socializing. Libelle Summer Week responds to this perfectly.

Below: A Dutch man on vacation, waiting outside the store.

ketplace. In the 1980s, it became clear that differences between people were becoming less and less physical and more of an emotional nature. As a response to this, techniques were developed whereby people could be categorized according to lifestyle, grouped according to shared core values. Based on models and supported by mood boards and storyboards, organizations tried to get a feeling for the specific target group. Although these techniques can contribute to consumer insight, the problem today is that they are now applied by most organizations, so that the various players within a given sector or product category will all reach similar outcomes. This means that sectors will transform as a whole, but that very little differentiation is achieved within the sector itself. For organizations, increasing competition and the ongoing battle for the attention of consumers, differentiation is becoming increasingly important. Because of this, more attention will have to be paid to deeper consumer insight that does justice to the dynamics of people's emotional lives. According to Stienstra, instead of simplifying reality, insight has to be gained into motivations, emotions, ideas and associations.

The more accurately this target group is described, the more effectively the brand and the products can be translated to fit the individual. By offering relevant and attractive products, and with a distinctive position and identity, a retail brand will appeal to a greater or lesser degree to specific groups of customers and be able to build on those relationships.

■ *Women love browsing and being surprised by what they encounter in a shop.*

SITUATIONS AND BEHAVIOUR

AS MENTIONED, PEOPLE ON HOLIDAY ARE IN A DIFFERENT STATE OF MIND THAN DURING AN AVERAGE WORKING WEEK.

In the photograph of a father and son in a shopping street, both are wearing shorts and short-sleeved shirts and look as though they have all the time in the world, just enjoying the sunshine. We can imagine that the mother and daughter in the store are also wearing summer clothes and are looking around in search of a new summer dress or bikini. It is not because they really need them, but just because they are looking to see if they can discover something new. They too will be looking around in a different way than they had two weeks before, back in the Netherlands getting ready for their holiday. At that point, they probably had the feeling that they had to succeed in finding what they needed in the clothing stores, because otherwise, they would not have had anything nice to wear during their holiday.

This is a fictitious example, but it shows that people are in different moods and have different attitudes and needs in different circumstances. A person is and remains the same person, but they adapt their behaviour to each new situation, making them different consumers. Where we have come to know about the average consumer and the motivations that drive every western individual, at the personal level, we see different segments and target groups.

People have unique personalities, each with their own personality traits. This individual identity is a permanent and unchangeable factor, but in our everyday lives, we have to adapt to and operate in so many different social situations that we change our behaviour accordingly. An individual has a very dynamic personality. This means that

people have different moods in the mornings than in the afternoons, that they feel differently on Mondays than on Saturdays and differently in spring than in the autumn. When they are on holiday, they relax more than when they are in the midst of the daily grind. People can feel differently at every hour of the day and they behave according to the way they feel.

For each distinct situation, our moods and behaviour will often be inconsistent, and at the same time, enormously divided. Someone can be very extroverted on one occasion, but crawl into their shell on another, behave differently in a group than when alone and differently again in the company of different people. This time, they may select healthy food, but they could equally well buy an unhealthy snack the next time. Sometimes, shopping has to be done as quickly and as efficiently as possible, but at other times, customers take their time and read all the information they can. People sometimes want food that is easy to prepare or (almost) ready to eat, and on other occasions, they indulge in culinary tours de force produced completely from scratch. Sometimes the price does not matter at all, and sometimes people change their minds over pennies.

Consumer behaviour changes every time they buy something. Someone's mood, the reason they visit the store, their age, their character and how well they know the store are all determining factors in how they shop and what they expect from the store. Moreover, shopping behaviour can change even within the short time they are in the store. A store will have to take all of these variables into account. No matter who the customer is, they will have an influence on him or her personally.

For each distinct situation, consumer moods and behaviour will often be inconsistent, and at the same time, enormously divided.

In the Moment-Mood Model© the four factors that influence customer and prospective customer behaviour come together. All four are related to one another because they continually influence each other. Sometimes one will have the upper hand (a cheerful mood that is simply indestructible, for example), sometimes several factors are 'active' and different desires and moods will continually alternate, because of different situations, for instance. The four factors mean the following:

NEED:
- Is a person actually intent on buying a particular product? Or is he just looking or shopping for fun or doing routine errands? Needs differ from one consumer to the next. Different needs often have to be catered for side by side within a store.

MOOD
- When someone is cheerful, he is receptive to very different things than when is depressed, stressed or sad. As a retailer you can capitalize upon alternating and very specific moods and try to influence buying behaviour. It shows that you understand your customer.

SITUATION
- Carefully arranging things for the consumer is often an excellent way of taking advantage of the situation. Through their journey through the store and a well thought-out service concept, for instance, but also by giving them just what they need at the right moment. That way you can surprise a person, hold their attention and exert a positive influence on their mood.

EXTERNAL INFLUENCES
- All sorts of outside influences can have an effect on ultimate behaviour and influence a person's mood or needs. The fact is, nothing can be done about these sorts of unpredictable factors. That is precisely the difference with situational factors, which can be influenced.

Customer behaviour can be better understood by acknowledging and recognizing these factors. Moreover, they also play a role in a customer's feeling of satisfaction or fulfilment after making a purchase. As you can probably imagine, a customer's good mood can turn into dejection if he becomes frustrated by a fruitless search for a particular product in a store. Or the other way around, if he has been helped more than expected because a member of the staff understood what he needed, he certainly will come back the next time.

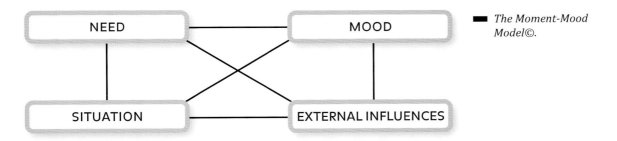

■ *The Moment-Mood Model©.*

■ *An advertisement on a London bus, which for many will hit a sensitive nerve. Smart advertising for a British magazine.*

THE PURPOSE OF SHOPPING

IDEO DESIGN STUDIO HAS ANALYSED THE SHOPPING NEEDS OF CONSUMERS. THEY HAVE DESCRIBED FIVE DIFFERENT SHOPPING MODES THAT MATCH THE GOAL THAT ONE HAS IN MIND WHEN SHOPPING:

MISSION MODE:
- Get in, get out, save as much time as possible.

RESTOCK MODE:
- Low emotional engagement; acting on autopilot, aimed at the specific product.

BACKGROUND MODE:
- The real purpose is not shopping, but something else, such as socializing. New information and inspiration are welcome here, but actual purchases are incidental. In this situation, a place to stop and eat supports the customers.

CELEBRATION MODE:
- Shopping as entertainment. Shoppers are out to enjoy themselves and want to be spoiled. New ideas and inspiration are very welcome, 'limited editions' even more so.

BEYOND-THE-STORE MODE:
- The shopper's thoughts are already focused on using the product. Shopping for a special occasion, such as a gala event, is a good example.

The reason someone visits a store determines how they shop and what they expect from the store.

■ *A shopping street has something for everyone.*

6.
BRANDING AND RETAIL BRANDING

Similarities and differences

ABOUT THE ORIGINS OF BRANDING, THE POWER OF BRANDS, THE INVOLVEMENT OF PEOPLE, THREE LAWS FOR SUCCESSFUL BRANDING, VISUAL IDENTITY, ABOUT WHAT RETAIL BRANDING IS, THE STORE AS A BRAND PLATFORM AND ABOUT THE CONTACT BETWEEN BRAND AND CONSUMER.

APPLE

*When we hear the word apple,
we do not just think about a piece of fruit.
That's the power of branding.*

102

■ *A brand makes a white polo shirt distinctive. The alligator is a recognizable Lacoste icon.*

BRANDS HELP CONSUMERS MAKE DECISIONS WITHIN AN ABUNDANT SUPPLY OF CHOICES. BRANDS ALSO HELP PEOPLE EXPRESS THEMSELVES AND BOLSTER THEIR IDENTITY AND STATUS.

Brands that have a clear identity and make clear statements and propositions of their own are more likely to be selected by consumers, because they can more easily identify with these brands and because it helps them back up their decision to purchase something. Companies with strong brands are therefore more successful, because these organizations have a distinct vision of the objectives they are striving to achieve and their own role in society. Why is this true, and how does this work? To find out, we will first go back to the beginning.

The rise of branding went hand in hand with the development of retail trade. When products were still being personally delivered to customers – by the farmers themselves, or by vendors and open-air markets – the person who made the product, bred the animals or grew the produce was directly connected to those products. This personal touch was what made people feel emotionally connected, and they developed a relationship with the supplier, a human relationship of reciprocity and trust. People clearly valued this relationship, and their loyalty was reinforced by positive experiences with the products and the contact with the seller.

The origins of branding are founded in this personal interaction. There was as yet no real form for consumers to recognize specific producers, such as a logo or some other kind of visual identity, and it was only for practical reasons that livestock breeders began branding their cattle and horses as a way of identifying the owners.

They then knew which animals belonged to whom when they were out grazing together and could identify the animals if they escaped or were stolen.

It did not take long, however, for potential buyers to identify these individual brands with specific qualities and identities of the breeders. This took on an increasingly important role when there were several breeders competing with one another. Thanks to this form of visual identification, specific, distinctive qualities could be associated with a given supplier, product or service. The principle underlying the branding of livestock was therefore gradually adopted by more and different trades.

Between those days of person-to-person transactions and the world we live in today, and under the influence of all kinds of factors, an enormous increase in scale has taken place, so that person-to-person selling has disappeared, making way for increasingly anonymous transactions. For this reason, other ways had to be found to communicate the personality, relevance, context and distinctive characteristics of any given supplier. 'Branding' became increasingly important and has now become professionalized. It serves to identify and convey the reputation of the manufacturer or producer.

The primary objective of branding, therefore, is that the product being supplied is able to go out into the world on its own, that it is recognized when it does so, able to communicate its qualities. It has to be striking enough to attract attention and be distinguishable, while on the other hand, it also has to connect with the personality traits of the given brand. In addition, branding is the binding factor between products of the same brand

at different locations and in different forms. The brand serves as the sender, a recognizable way to locate something in a busy street, in a section of a supermarket or on the web, and it serves as an enticement that can persuade consumers to make a purchase.

The origins of branding are founded in this personal interaction.

■ *Branding has its origins in the branding of cattle, which soon became a mark of quality.*

WHAT BRANDING IS

BRANDING COMES FROM THE ACTIVE VERB, 'TO BRAND'. BRANDING COMPRISES ALL THE ACTIVITIES THAT AN ORGANIZATION UNDERTAKES TO BRING THEIR BRANDS AND PRODUCTS INTO THE MINDS OF CONSUMERS, GIVING THESE BRANDS AND PRODUCTS THE ABILITY TO ACTIVELY PARTICIPATE IN THE MARKETPLACE.

The organization continually works at keeping the brand relevant to the spirit of the times in a given society. This calls for an emotional interaction between the brand and consumers, one that leads to consumer loyalty. After all, if consumers do not feel any bond with a brand, it does not necessarily mean that they will no longer purchase that brand, but it does mean that their attention can easily be distracted by the competition. If a competitor does succeed in creating such a bond with consumers, those consumers can only be won back with a great deal of effort. In retail, it is the survival of the fittest, and 'fittest' refers to the ability to win customers through seduction. The game being played here is about conveying the brand as genuinely and realistically as possible. The company expresses its identity and ambitions in the form of promises that have to be continually kept in order to retain consumer loyalty and ensure that the image of the brand continues to reflect that identity. For this reason, in branding, it is true that organizations have to be able to focus on both the short term and the long term. Broad contours have to be defined and followed, while in the short term, people still have to respond to external influences that affect the image of the brand, and with it, customer loyalty.

Branding represents the identity and ambition of the company in the spirit of its day.

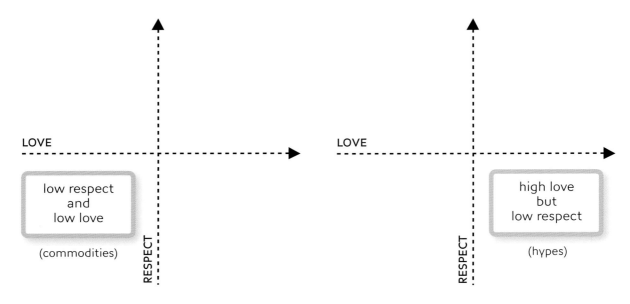

■ *Four types of brands according to Kevin Roberts in his book 'Lovemarks'.*

LOVE

low respect
and
low love

RESPECT

(commodities)

LOVE

high love
but
low respect

RESPECT

(hypes)

106

THE POWER OF BRANDING

Both the strength and the weakness of branding lie in the link that connects identity and image, the connection between personification of the brand and real people, between rationality and emotion. This is a sensitive and powerful concept that is sometimes difficult to comprehend in the context of our rationalized world, in which everything has to be measurable, cost-conscious and commercial. There are extremely 'soft' elements in the structure of a brand, because they have to be able to forge connections with real people, people who are not rational, but impulsive and intuitive. After the fact, people are inclined to explain why they buy certain brands or products – and in which store – based on rational characteristics or ideas. These reasons are intended to make them come across as sober, rational buyers with real understanding of what is going on. In truth, we do not have such profound understanding of most things. What do I really know about flowers or goat's cheese, about cars or facial creams? In any case, I certainly do not know everything about all of them. Even if I did, my emotions would still have the upper hand. I know that I cannot taste any difference between water from my kitchen sink and Bling H2O, but if I want to make an occasion special, I could well be tempted to pay € 35 for a bottle of Bling, even if, looking at it rationally, I know there is a very good chance that, with the exception of the price and the design of the bottle, there is nothing special at all about Bling H2O. Such is the power of branding.

It is a power that never fails to work. Every time we make a choice, between comparable stores, products or services, our (subconscious) preference will lean toward certain brands.
This preference is based, amongst other things, on experience, on what others have told us, the

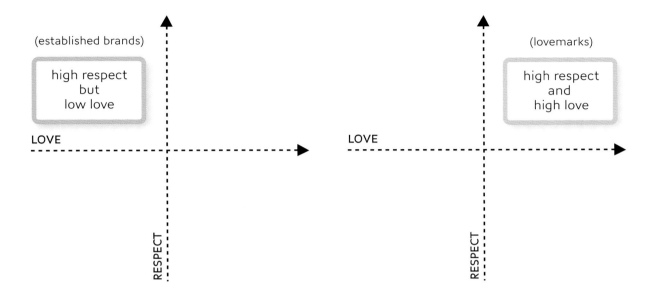

status of the brand and the type of purchase, as well as the opportunity to purchase and make use of the product. In his book, Lovemarks, Kevin Roberts describes how preferences for and evaluation of brands actually work. By dividing factors across different axes, the degree of respect for a brand is juxtaposed against the degree of love for that same brand. Using this comparison, Roberts goes on to define four types of brands. He begins with commodities, goods that are generally common property, which command little respect and almost no love. The second type includes brands for which there is a great deal of love, but little respect. These are the novelties, the whims and fads, which are generally doomed to a very brief existence. The third are the brands that are highly respected, but that people are not in love with. These are often major brands, brands that stay with us our whole lives, but which do not really touch us.

The last group is what Roberts refers to as the 'Lovemarks': brands for which people have respect as well as real love, and which they would not want to do without in their lives.

It used to be that a high level of respect was enough. Today, more is needed. Because of the extensive selections of products and services available to us, and also because we are very self-reliant and focused on self-realization, we want brands to make a real contribution to our lives. There has to be a real spark between a product and a user, one that is deeply rooted in the minds and hearts of people. When this happens, people are strongly devoted to a brand. For this to happen, the brand has to bind consumers to its personality and fulfil the promise made by the brand. The brand (the store, the product, the service, etc.) has to have something that makes a lasting impression and is truly distinctive, something that people want to tell others about. This is how we can guarantee and build on the loyalty of our customers. Jim Stolze talks about expressing this love in a more active form: in terms of giving attention. In his book, Uitverkocht (Sold Out), Stolze explains that the most valuable thing a brand can do is earn the interest of consumers. This is the way a brand can distinguish itself in an overcrowded market in which almost everything is available and consumers already have everything. It is about attracting that consumer's attention, winning a moment in their busy schedules. Every single day, because they have to manage their time, consumers must set priorities. It is wonderful when a brand can be so high on that list of priorities that the customer comes to you, or even stands in line waiting for a store to open when a new product is launched.

"Gaining the consumer's attention is the most valuable thing for a brand; a moment in his or her busy schedule."

JIM STOLZE

This reminds us of trying to get tickets to a rock concert, fans in sleeping bags lined up in front of the ticket agencies, or huddled over their computers in the early hours for a chance to order tickets online. The degree to which people love and give their attention to a brand can also lead to their becoming true fans. They are so enthusiastic about the brand that they make their enthusiasm widely known, sharing it with others, providing their own word-of-mouth advertising, telling all their friends and acquaintances about it through online social networks. For brands, fans are infinitely valuable and powerful, because their involvement with the brand leads to their becoming ambassadors, trying to convince others of that brand's added value. Here, they are attempting to persuade others to become fans as well, because they would like to have kindred spirits with whom they can share their passion.

"Relevance, coherence and participation are required for successful branding."

TJACO H. WALVIS

As we already know, the value attributed to the recommendations of others is perhaps greater than that attributed to what the brand itself communicates. When fans talk about a brand like this, with so much passion, those fans need to be cherished. Moreover, it is worth our while to investigate how we can better use them as ambassadors for our brand. To do this, we have to tap into and exploit that positive energy – the thing that the fans appreciate most – and offer them a platform where the brand and the fans can interact, and where fans can interact amongst themselves.

Involvement at this level can make fans feel as though they are part owners of that brand. Then, if there is some kind of change made, for example, to the logo of 'their' brand, they will take it to heart. When IKEA decided to change their house style font from Futura and Century Schoolbook to Verdana, a whole community of typography lovers rose up in protest. They believed Verdana

GAP redesigned its logo. Masses of people sent in what they thought were better alternatives. The change was soon reversed.

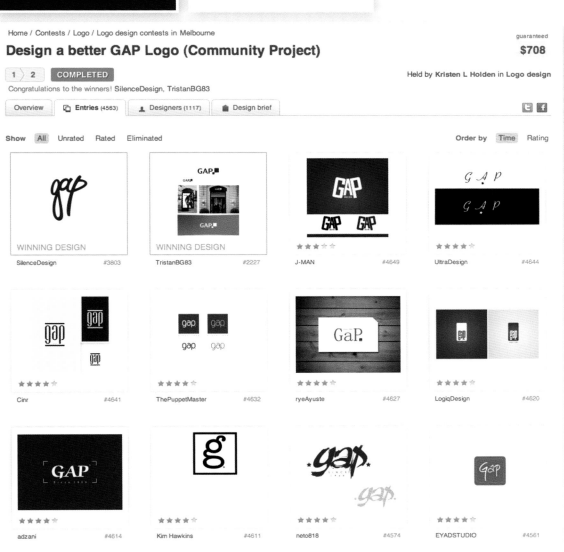

was designed for functionality and had low aesthetic value, and that it was unsuitable for printing. When GAP wanted to change its logo, countless graphic designers sent them alternative logos at no cost. Competitions and discussions were organized to convince the management of GAP to change their minds. There was even widespread speculation that this had been a strategic move by GAP, specifically intended to make consumers more involved with the brand. That might have been a very clever strategy, but it proved not to be the case. A similar discussion arose with the new Starbucks logo. Social media naturally provide a perfect platform for people to express their opinions and concerns and to find others who feel the same, so that they encourage one another.

It would seem that people are by nature averse to change. This is even truer in the case of a 'Lovemark' brand. It has to be said, however, that people become accustomed to the change quickly, and they no longer want to return to the way things had been.

> *"A major trend (in branding) in the coming period will be relevance. Your brand may look good, but what's in it for me? What is the relevance for your customers?"*
>
> **ANDY PAYNE, GLOBAL CHIEF CREATIVE OFFICER OF INTERBRAND**

LIVING THE BRAND

IN KEEPING WITH DEVELOPMENTS IN RETAIL, IT IS ALSO TRUE OF BRANDING THAT IT IS NO LONGER SO MUCH ABOUT THE PARTICULAR STRENGTHS OF THE BRAND ITSELF, BUT INCREASINGLY ABOUT THE RELEVANCE AND MEANING THAT THESE STRENGTHS HAVE IN THE MINDS OF CONSUMERS.

Brands had been accustomed to defining their 'unique selling points' and using these as the foundation of their communications. Today, they have to shift to 'unique buying reasons'. Because of the enormous overloading of the marketplace and the 'push' behaviour of suppliers, a 'pull' strategy will become increasingly important. This will quickly turn into an interactive relationship with clients and customers. A brand is no longer something that just belongs to the supplier – it belongs every bit as much to the recipient. Websites such as I Hate Starbucks show us that customers have opinions and freely communicate those opinions, be it by way of a website of this kind or by way of all kinds of social networks. An organization can achieve successful branding by complying with three laws of branding.

In the interaction between the brand and the consumer, the brand has to show its human side. To engage in valuable interaction, the real identity and bandwidth of the brand has to be made clearly visible. Within this bandwidth, the brand must then anticipate the various situations in which it will be operating. By tailoring the way it behaves in response to given situations, time and again, the brand will be relevant and have meaning for consumers. According to Tjaco H. Walvis, this is the first law of branding: providing distinctive relevance. The brand has to connect to the needs and the identity of the consumers, so that consumers can recognize themselves in it and it complements their self-image. The greater the number of relevant aspects associated with the brand, the greater the likelihood that it will become engraved in people's memories.

In his study, 'Three Laws of Branding: Neuroscientific Foundations of Effective Brand Building', Walvis cites two additional golden rules for successful branding. Number two is the importance of coherence, which means that over a longer period, all the expressions and actions of the brand remain cohesive and interconnected. This does not mean that you have to keep doing the same thing or repeat yourself. What it is about is that the essence and the style remain consistent, that the producer continues to be recognizable. Everything the brand does, and is, reinforces everything else. One example of a strong, coherent brand is Armani, who has turned a clothing brand into a lifestyle brand. At the Armani flagship store in Milan, Armani fans can of course find clothing and perfumes, but they also see his interior collection, books, a coffee shop, bonbons, a restaurant, a whole floor of Sony products and even his own flower selections. These flowers in particular are a fantastic

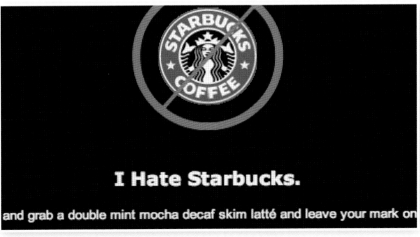

■ *Starbucks has fans and haters. Both express themselves through social media.*

111

example of what clever branding can achieve. We can all vividly imagine the situation: a woman stops in to visit her friend and observes, 'Oh, aren't those tulips beautiful!', to which her friend then proudly replies, 'Yes, aren't they? They are Armani.' Then you know that this is a very, very strong brand.

Another clever move on the part of Armani is the Sony floor. In addition to being an interesting form of co-branding, this department also serves another purpose. People can play computer games, watch television on gigantic flat screens and try out the newest products. It is a paradise and a hangout for young people who do not yet have enough money to purchase the products, but they come anyway, and they have good experiences. Armani will now be permanently engraved in their minds. In this way, Armani is subtly generating goodwill with the younger generation, and when that generation is a little older and does have money, they will continue to come back and will (hopefully) be purchasers.

The third law of branding is participation. Brands that invite people to actively engage with them have a greater chance of success. This law emphasizes the importance of physical and mental inter-

action within the total context of the brand. An example of this is Legoland. In these stores, children can test their parts and models before they are purchased. The power of this concept becomes even clearer when we look at the countless Lego fan clubs. These clubs are made up of organized groups of adults and children who, sometimes individually, sometimes collectively, experiment with the possibilities that the Lego pieces offer. In this way, Lego users motivate one another to create highly advanced structures and projects. They use the products in their most ad-

An example of a strong, coherent brand is Armani, now a rich lifestyle brand.

vanced form, so that Lego in turn learns from its fan club. Where consumer insight and strategic development are concerned, Lego fans are a direct and therefore extremely valuable and practical source of ideas for the Lego organization.

Apple also has very high regard for participation. Apple stores are always full of people who are trying out and using Apple products. This is also the Apple approach: a salesperson does not immediately approach you. Instead, you have all the freedom and time you want to remain in the store. By creating this experience of user convenience, Apple ultimately generates sales as well as fans. In both their stores and online, they also offer a range of workshops to help people get the most out of their products, so that you – the consumer – can get maximum enjoyment from them. This same approach also underscores the apps for the iPhone and the iPad: the software is relatively simple, so that the apps can easily be developed and made widely available. Users can then put together their own apps packages, so they can perfectly customize the functionality of their iPhones and iPads to suit their own personal needs.

The effect of (retail) branding is that a whole world opens up for you when you see, experience, or even think of the brand.

VISUAL IDENTITY

AS WE HAVE MENTIONED, THE OBJECTIVE OF BRANDING IS THAT THE PRODUCT BEING OFFERED CAN GO OUT INTO THE WORLD ON ITS OWN, AND BE RECOGNIZED, ITS QUALITIES COMMUNICATED TO THE WORLD.

The way to do this is visual identity. Visual identity makes a product or service visible and its provider (the brand) recognizable. This involves more than a logo and house style, more than a stamp or a trademark. Visual identity represents what the company stands for and what it believes. The whole combination of name, logo, typography, colour and visual language reveal this heart and vision of the brand. It is in the blending of these elements and the selected style, colour, character, with their collected symbolic meaning, that the identity is made visible. This can be so powerful that when it is visualized in another language, the brand is still immediately recognized.

Imagine walking through a completely strange city, where you cannot read the language and do not understand what is written on the signs. The minute you see a certain familiar yellow 'M', you immediately know what it will look like inside, what you will be able to eat there, more or less what it will cost and how fast the service is going to be. You can even anticipate the sense of guilt you will have after eating a McMenu meal. Because the combination of elements is so strong in the minds of consumers, they can see from any single one of these elements that it immediately refers to that particular brand. We might also think of the Nike Swoosh.

When we recognize a brand, it will evoke the same feelings we had in our earlier experiences with that brand. This recognition also evokes

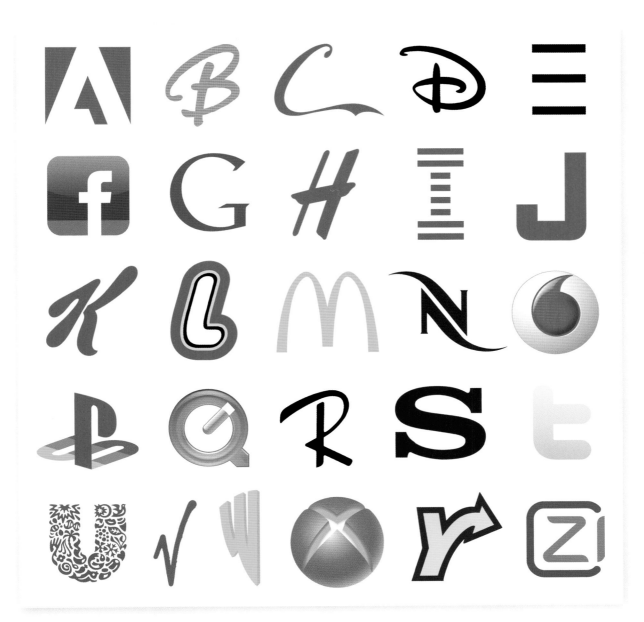

■ *With a good visual identity, seeing just part of it triggers the brand association. From top to bottom: Adobe, Barbie, Coca-Cola, Disney, Esprit, Facebook, Google, H&M, IBM, JVC, Kellogg's, Lego, McDonalds, Nespresso, Vodafone, Playstation, Quicktime, Ray-Ban, Sony, Twitter, Unilever, Virgin, Warner Bros, Xbox, Subways, Ziggo.*

certain expectations, which have to be met each time the brand is experienced. These expectations are brand specific: in the Dutch Albert Heijn supermarkets, in terms of service, price and quality, customers have different expectations than they do at Aldi supermarkets. We also have different expectations of a house brand than we do of an A-brand.

The power of the elements of a visual identity to be recognizable is a necessity, a prerequisite. Because of growing competition and the huge amounts of information that consumers are confronted with every day, their attention becomes increasingly selective. They rely more on symbols when making their choices. One can say that more than ever before, we live in a visual communications society. People do not have enough time and patience and have therefore become highly skilled in absorbing and understanding iconography: characters and symbols. As soon as we see an image, a whole world opens up to us. A visual brand identity therefore has to carry weight and have meaning for consumers. To achieve this, it is essential to maintain recognizability and consistency for years at a time. Only the drops of water that continue to fall in the very same place on a stone succeed in carving their way into the stone. It is an old saying, but it applies here. At the same time, the entire brand needs to evolve and gain depth as it adapts to time and the spirit of its day. In this sense, seeing a visual identity as an icon is too static and immovable. We therefore require the necessary freedom in how we use visual identity. What is most important, however, is that the brand remains easily recognizable, that it is understood as it is meant to be understood. The individual elements of a visual identity do not just assume meaning from one day to the next: it all needs time and focus.

■ *If the combination of elements in a visual identity is strongly loaded in the minds of consumers, seeing just one of these elements immediately evokes the brand. Above: IKEA in Dubai. Below: McDonalds in Marrakech.*

■ *Nike uses its swoosh in a new composition for its own sub-label.*

A visual identity doesn't assume meaning from one day to the next. It all needs time and focus.

WHAT RETAIL BRANDING IS

THE MAJOR DIFFERENCE BETWEEN RETAIL BRANDS AND MANUFACTURERS' BRANDS IS THAT WITH RETAIL BRANDS, THERE IS DIRECT INTERACTION BETWEEN CONSUMERS AND THE COMPANY OR PRODUCT.

In contrast, people working with manufacturers' brands do not come into direct contact with the end users, because the retail channels stand between the two. Nor is the factory accessible to the consumers. Since there is no one-to-one contact, manufacturers' brands are in many cases anonymous or even fictitious suppliers. It is perfectly possible to think up a brand identity for a product, place it before a specific target group and then introduce it to consumers. Consider, for example, the completely different identities of Coca Cola, Dr Pepper, Sprite and Fanta, all of which are manufactured by the Coca-Cola Company.

The physical space of a store offers a retail brand the possibility of communicating with consumers, literally and figuratively, at the moment when the consumers are making their purchases. In this context, retailers have a one-to-one relationship with their customers.

This relationship is an open one, because in the store, retailers allow people to see their entire operation: it is impossible for them to hide. Every day, a retail brand has to be in good order, in all of its facets, including ambience, visual merchandising, assortment, product quality, level of service, price and staff. After all, inside the store, the entire set of values is experienced at a glance, scanned and judged by its visitors. This is where consumers (subconsciously) decide whether they want to bond with the brand or not. They will definitely know whether everything is as it should be, whether the brand is authentic and has an appealing character. As an illustration, when they hang the words, 'So Hip It Hurts', in great big letters on their store front on opening day, an organization presents a very strong brand image to the outside world. People will have high expectations when they enter the store. Inside, if everything they see does not look hip and the staff seem bored and disinterested, they will be disappointed. The promise they were made outside has not been kept inside. In retail branding, it is about attracting attention and being distinctive, then engaging people with an appropriate and authentic personality.

Another characteristic of retail branding is that a retailer is in principle neutral, because the decision to choose a product with a manufacturer's brand or a store's own brand is ultimately left to the shopper. A retailer helps consumers, because he has the opportunity to make a pre-selection and present this to potential customers in a transparent way (or indeed, in his own specific way). Given the selection, it is now left to the desires and the budget of the shopper: will he choose a premium brand or the house brand, a bag of prewashed lettuce leaves or a whole head of lettuce? Every product has its own price tag, but consumers are free to choose what they wish.

Once a consumer gets to know a retailer, trusts the quality of that retailer's selection and has built up good memories of visits to the store, the foundation has been laid for a long-term relationship, which can eventually lead to store loyalty. This is because retail branding creates brand preferences that reach beyond the products or service being offered. In other words, people first choose the store, then once in the store, they decide which product or brand they will purchase.

"You can sell a product or service by making it appear more attractive than it is – but not a company."

GIJS TEN KATE TEN KATE & PARTNERS, MANAGEMENT CONSULTING

People first decide to shop at supermarket Albert Heijn or C1000, and only then do they decide whether they buy Douwe Egberts coffee or the store brand coffee.

We refer to a strong retail brand when the store where a product is purchased plays an important role for the consumer, when a retail brand offers added value to the products that are sold there. Sephora is an example of a strong retail brand. This cosmetics chain sells all the major brands, complemented with their own product line of soaps, lipsticks and so on. Here, products by the major couturiers and perfumeries, including Guerlin, Armani, Chanel and Dolce & Gabbana, are all sold, and in such a convincing way that you are not just buying Armani or Chanel, but Armani or Chanel from Sephora. The ambiance, the presentation, the role of the staff, the service and the authority conveyed by the knowledge and the assortment are so perfect and overwhelming that this retail brand rises above even the strongest product brands.

Today, we also see a further development, as manufacturing brands are themselves seeking direct contact with their customers. They are developing stores of their own – temporary or otherwise,

The promise made outside the store must
be kept inside. Expectations for this store
in London's Camden Town are high.

because a shop of their own offers the perfect
platform to demonstrate what the brand stands
for. Given the increased numbers of manufacturers who are establishing their own retail locations, it seems that more and more brands are
understanding the advantages this has to offer.

*Retail is true democracy:
in the store, consumers are
free to choose whatever
product they want.*

Temporary stores are primarily in the form of
'pop-up' or 'guerrilla' stores. Their existence is
usually also accompanied by all the requisite cla-
mour. The aim here is primarily to draw attention
to the brand, with all due focus on the principles
of retail. The brand is able to demonstrate everything it has to offer, and it is also able to engage in
direct contact with its purchasers. This intensifies
the relationship between the brand and the customer. The temporary character of the store now
serves to give people who were there and made
purchases a sense of exclusivity: it was a unique
experience.

The permanent stores of manufacturers are also
not without their benefits. There are extremely

strong examples of retailers who began as manufacturers, including Nespresso and G-star. Because these are vertically integrated organizations, they hold all the various aspects of managing their companies firmly in their own hands, from production, to distribution, to the floor of the retail outlet. As we saw in the Platform Development Model©, this controlled and integrated approach is an exceedingly effective way of realizing a store formula.

In addition, the internet and social media offer new possibilities for creating contact with customers. Through social media, a dialogue can be established and a brand can better get to know its customers and their needs. Online marketing campaigns can be tried out in order to reinforce this relationship. For manufacturing brands, the advantage of this, compared to having a physical store of their own, is in the way the sale is made. It most closely resembles how products are sold through retailers. In this regard, the company is already orientated towards distribution, but there will now be streams of smaller quantities made available to individuals who move through this process. If we look at the Platform Development Model©, in the case of a webshop, not all of the parts are active, just as not all of the parts are active with the presence of a brand in a physical store. When a brand operates a store of its own,

this does have to be the case. In this sense, having a webshop of your own is relatively easy for manufacturers, because it is still true that not all the aspects of the company have to be revealed, and the manufacturers' brand can keep its anonymous or fictitious source. But beware: this is true as things stand today. Webshops are still relatively functionally organized, in the form of a database, as it were. We do not yet know how this is going to develop as time goes on, but we do know that more and more experience will continue to be added to enhance internet and webshops.

Today, people are making considerable effort to translate the strengths of the physical store to the webshops. One of the plus points of shopping streets is their social aspect, all the other people around you and shopping together with friends or family. Online, more and more tools are being developed to incorporate this aspect. One example of this is Wehkamp, who have integrated social and inspirational shopping into their website. Through their webshop, you are put in contact with friends who also happen to be online at the same time. You then navigate together through the site, with the same screens, seeing the same products. This way, you can discuss whether you want to buy the product or not. While you are shopping online, you can also employ a range of tools that offer advice and inspiration about style.

In addition, there are many more specifically focused possibilities with mobile internet. On the basis of the GPS location of a potential customer, a brand can make suggestions and offer ideas to customers who are in a physical shopping street. Staying with the example of Wehkamp, they launched an app that gave customers extra discounts when they purchased through their webshop. This is how it worked: when a consumer's GPS

Retail branding creates brand preferences that rise above the product or service being offered.

■ *A store is a place where passions are shared.
This is an Apple store and you can see that a
certain kind of people come and buy here.*

location indicated that he was in, for example, a
Mediamarkt store, a message was sent to his
smartphone saying that if he were to purchase an
electronic product through Wehkamp (i.e. not at
the Mediamarkt), a 10% discount would be available. Wehkamp also held a summer campaign, in
a less aggressive form. Beachgoers received pop-
ups on their smart phones with offers to purchase
swimwear at sizeable discounts. This pop-up was
only sent to people who were actually at the
beach at that moment. The relevance of the moment, the specific focus, which bring with them a
sense of exclusivity, make this a successful and
effective method of customer contact. The customer is already in the right frame of mind, and the

*"A relationship is created
when a retail space
ceases to be merely a
merchandising outlet and
instead becomes a place
where passion is shared."*

JEAN-NOËL KAPFERER

brand just gives him or her that extra little push. The potential that the digital world offers will no doubt mean that the power of retail branding will take on different dimensions. In any case, it will bring increasing competition. Branding will become more important for the entire customer journey, because it will not be only through mass media communications and in the stores themselves that customers can be inspired or tempted to make purchases. Certainly with mobile internet, consumers can decide to make a purchase whenever they want, using their phones and webshops.

RETAIL BRANDING DURING THE CUSTOMER JOURNEY

Retail branding is not only about the physical or virtual store, about the moment that the consumer is already visiting the store. Before that, it is about the path that takes them there and the choices they are faced with along the way. To take a look at this, we return here to the flower market we visited in Chapter 5, where it was easy to have an overview of the products for sale and where there are shared characteristics between different sellers. Here, the price, appearance and style of the vendor will be a determining factor for consumers. In a shopping street, the set of available choices is more difficult to bring together. It takes consumers more effort to discover whether a certain store connects to them, their desires and frame of mind, because they first have to go into the store. In this setting, you are very unlikely to walk from flower shop to flower shop in order to compare six different stores, something that is simple to do at an open-air market. For this reason, a store must immediately spark the interest of a consumer (or already be known to him or

her) before they take the trouble to actually go in. A retailer therefore has to ask customers to pay attention to him or her. That initial contact comes about through out-of-store communications, followed by the physical store and the look & feel of the whole. At an open-air market, a seller can look people in the eye, make a joke, extol the qualities of his products. In short, he can seek immediate contact.

The outdoor market and the high street both resemble a rocket with two stages: they first attract attention, then engage and create a bond with people through personality. The difference lies in the way that attention is drawn or attracted. At an open-air market, a vendor can do this directly, with his own personality. A store is only able to reveal that personality at a later stage. Indeed, the 'bonding' (with the 'market stall and seller', or with the store brand) can only take place when the personality that people discover there actually matches their own personalities.

> *A store has to stand out, draw attention and attract, then fulfil its promise with a real personality.*

A retailer must attract attention and use personality to create a bond. This vendor at Crawford Market in Mumbai India looks friendly.

Prof. Rob van der Kind has developed a theory that is partly based on this principle. A retailer, he proposes, can only achieve turnover if he has first attracted the attention of consumers by way of the external marketing mix. The external marketing mix is directed at sparking interest in the formula. On the one hand, (mass media) communications need to be complete, focused at brand awareness and image. On the other hand, the story itself has to possess stopping power, through the shop front, windows, logo, location and so on (around-the-store communication). He calls this the attraction value of the store formula, comparable to the principle that if it is going to get customers to come inside at all, the store must first and foremost attract, be striking and appealing.

> *"It is no longer about stimulating and creating a bond. Your brand appeal also has to be carried through internally. If your staff do not radiate this appeal, how can you expect consumers ever to pick it up?"*

**ERIK SAELENS MANAGING DIRECTOR
BRANDHOME.COM**

The second part of the turnover is achieved by means of the internal marketing mix (the transaction value): translating the interest already kindled into actual purchasing behaviour. This means that inside the store, everything has to be as it should be: assortment, visual merchandising, the store design and interior, and the intangible elements, such as ambience and perception. Staff are important here too. They are in direct contact with consumers and are close to the products they are offering. Whether staff are friendly and helpful, young and hip, or indeed, almost invisible, makes a major difference in how people experience a store, and this can be directly measured in cash register receipts. People working in the store are in this sense the real personification of the brand, and they are very strong determining factors in retail branding. They have to make the promises come true.

By combining the attraction value with the transaction value, we can build a formula for the turnover (T):

$$T = CA \times TI \times C \times TP$$

The catchment area (CA) and the turn-out index (TI) determine the attraction value. The conversion (C) and ticket price (TP) are the transaction value.

To clarify the power of the proportional increase, the positive influences of both components have a reinforcing effect on one another. Turning this around, underemphasizing either one of the two components can cancel out the (positive) effect of the other. The same rules of the game that apply to branding in general also apply to retail branding. The extra dimension, however, is the direct contact with the customer and the openness in the relationship that this entails. The effects of retail branding are immediately measured in sales results. For this reason, they can also be quickly adjusted, so that people's image of the brand continues to be the same as the brand identity. The design of the store and in-store communications are becoming increasingly important, because one-to-one contact is becoming a greater determinant for how a consumer or a customer experiences and judges the brand: the image of the brand. Employees therefore have to conform to that personality, culture and organizational orientation. After all, the staff are the brand.

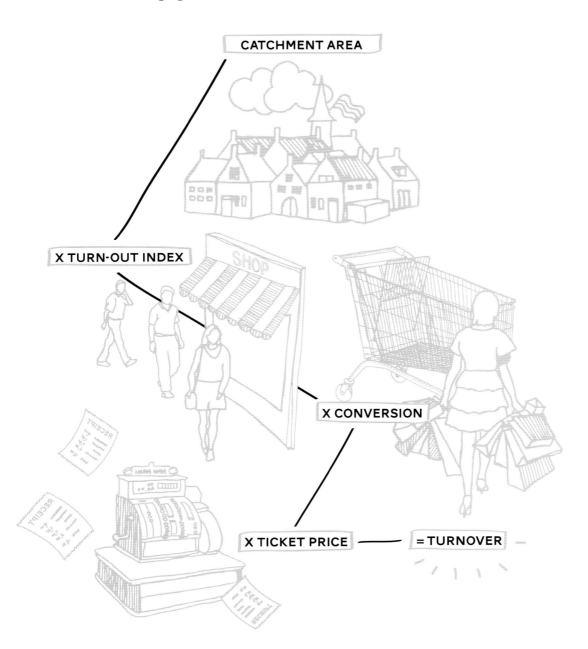

CATCHMENT AREA

X TURN-OUT INDEX

X CONVERSION

X TICKET PRICE ——— = TURNOVER

7.
RETAIL BRAND DEVELOPMENT

Building the foundation of the retail formula

ABOUT BRAND IDENTITY AND BRAND IMAGE, HOW THEY WORK IN RETAIL, A BRAND AS A QUALITY LABEL AND STATUS SYMBOL, THE ROLE OF THE ORGANIZATION, ABOUT DEFINING THE BRAND IDENTITY, POSITIONING AND AMBITIONS, PROTECTING A BRAND AND ABOUT DIFFERENT TYPES OF BRAND ARCHITECTURE AND RETAIL BRAND ARCHETYPES.

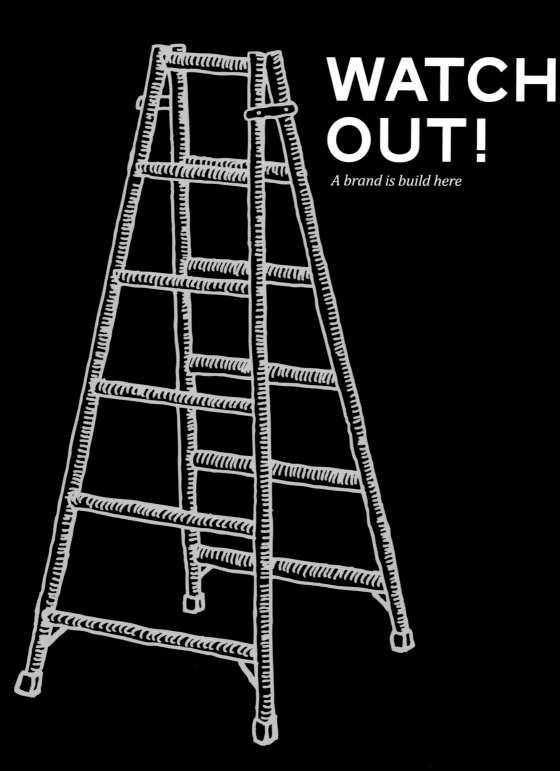

WATCH OUT!

A brand is build here

128

■ *Burberry has evolved its brand wonderfully. Now, it attracts a younger audience but retains its existing customers.*

STRONG, SUCCESSFUL BRANDS HAVE TO BE AUTHENTIC. DEVELOPING SUCH A BRAND DOES NOT HAPPEN OVERNIGHT. IT REQUIRES A GREAT DEAL OF ATTENTION AND TIME. THE BRAND HAS TO BE WELL BUILT, FROM THE FOUNDATION TO THE FINAL STRUCTURE.

If a brand has been around for a while, but has lost strength and relevance, then it is also necessary to investigate the foundations and, where necessary, repair them. Only then can one begin building again. Otherwise, things get messy and unstable, or worse: the structure collapses. A brand therefore has to have a solid foundation, and it has to be integrated into the operations of the enterprise, so that it can be expressed clearly and recognizably in all the activities of the organization.

Within organizations, people often take the importance of careful brand development too lightly. In many cases, only certain departments really have a grip on the brand, even though the brand or brands sold by the company actually embody the values of the enterprise. Products and services can be purchased everywhere, at every price, so why do people purchase them from brand A and not brand B?

"You have to define the foundation to begin with. You clean up the rubble, get the foundation right, and then you can build."

**VITTORIO RADICE
FORMER CEO, SELFRIDGES**

To underscore the importance of brands, each year, Interbrand compiles an assessment of the book values of different brands. In addition, since 2009, Interbrand has also reported on the 50 most valuable retail brands. Because these assessments are repeated annually, they provide an insight into which marketing strategies are the most effective. These reports leave little doubt that the leaders in the retail sector are all strongly market orientated, that they have clear insight into the world and the lives of consumers and set their marketing strategy accordingly.

> *"Marketing communicates quickly and single-mindedly; branding is slow and multi-faceted."*

JACQUES CHEVRON, FOUNDER JCR&A

BRAND IDENTITY AND BRAND IMAGE

A BRAND IS TWO THINGS IN ONE. IT IS THE INSIDE, REPRESENTING THE TRUE IDENTITY OF AN ORGANIZATION, TRANSLATED INTO A SET OF UNDERLYING RATIONAL AND EMOTIONAL VALUES. THE BRAND IDENTITY DESCRIBES WHO OR WHAT THE BRAND IS.

A brand is formed by the combination of DNA, positioning in the market and ambitions, all of which flow seamlessly into one another and have long-term relevance. As Jacques Chevron, founder of JCR&A, has said, 'Marketing communicates quickly and single-mindedly; branding is slow and multifaceted.' In other words: branding is not marketing. It is not a house style or a payoff, but is the basis and the future of the organization. As such, it is also a motivator, the source of inspiration. The brand identity offers the organization a solid grip and direction in everything it does, while binding employees together because they are all aiming to achieve the same ambitions. It is multilayered, and it is comprised of many components that must be integrated and work together. It is the core from which the brand communicates and develops itself.

Ultimately, the brand exists in the eyes of the marketplace. It is the market that determines the image, the outside: what people see, what they appreciate, what they detest or simply could not care less about. This will depend on the context and the relevance with which the encounter with the market takes place. This context applies to both the specific situation and to the general spirit of the times, while relevance is not simply about what is being offered within that context, but about how it is being offered and by whom.

For a consumer, a brand is a mark of quality of the supplier, who generates trust that it will be good. The brand also says something about the people who use it. They identify with the values of the brand, which connect to their own identity or desired status. They are always – consciously or unconsciously – asking themselves such questions as, 'What does it say about me when I buy this or that?', 'Does this brand give me the right status?', 'Is this the store where I want to be seen?' and so on. Through the brands they buy, they can demonstrate to the outside world who they are, what their tastes are, what their limits are and where they belong. A brand therefore serves as an expression of style, or in fact, lifestyle.

"Customers don't choose products on the basis of price or effectiveness; instead they ask themselves: what sort of dinner set defines me as a person?"

NARRATOR IN THE MOVIE 'FIGHT CLUB'

■ *Shopping bags are an important element of branding and a clear visual identity is essential. They enable people to show their fellow consumers where they have shopped and what they can afford. This man has just been to Saks Fifth Avenue in New York City.*

BRAND IDENTITY AND BRAND IMAGE IN RETAIL

The Retail Formula© model visualizes the trajectory between the identity of a retailer and the retailer's image in the market. At the top of the model, we find the identity, composed of a rational segment and an emotional segment. The rational applies to what it is and how it works, while the emotional applies to who the supplier is and what that means to you as a buyer. At the bottom of the model is the image, or how you are perceived by the market. We could say that the formula for success lies somewhere between these two extremes.

When we look at identities, it appears that organizations often forget about the emotional segment. When retailers list their strengths (their Unique Selling Propositions, or USPs), they usually only refer to the Rational Selling propositions, or RSPs, which are in many cases things that can be copied, while a consumer primarily makes a decision to become a customer or not, or to remain a customer on the grounds of emotions, or non-rational reasons.

You can, for example, be the first to come up with hip, orange T-shirts, but there is a good chance that within two weeks, the whole street will be selling orange T-shirts. How do you manage to get shoppers to buy that T-shirt from you, and not from one of the others? The crux of the matter lies in the added value, something that is added to the shirt itself, an extra value that derives from the combination of the product (or the service) and the personality. This is the fingerprint of the organization. It is what distinguishes the T-shirt from those of the other sellers. It is therefore worthwhile to get a good grasp of the emotional side of a company and communicate this, both externally and internally.

The brand concept is developed from the identity (with the emotional and rational values), the positioning and the ambition, or market vision. It is the starting point for the formula, the reach of the brand and the organization. With a successful formula, all of the expressions of the brand come from a single source. The entire organization lives and breathes the brand. The brand concept takes shape in the formula elements, which form a bridge to the image. If the translation of the brand concepts into all the formula elements is right, the image is the same as your identity, because consumers then pick up the right values.

In retail, customers stay in stores longer if they feel that the brand matches their own identity, so that the brand gives their identity added value. The experience of being in the store is then a more pleasant one, and these customers will return to these stores more frequently. It is often possible to say that certain kinds of people visit and purchase things in certain stores. Borrowing a term used in psychology, introduced by the German psychologists Wolfgang Köhler and Max Wertheimer, this is referred to as Gestalt. Gestalt is the idea that the whole is more than the sum of the parts: a table is more than four legs and a board across the top; human personality is more than the total of the traits that can be described and measured. Likewise, a brand radiates out to all the customers who come along, but each type of customer also radiates onto the personality of the brand. The result is that some people feel more attracted to a brand and others do not. This again irrefutably underscores the importance of having deep insight into the world of the customer: what he longs for, aspires to and experiences as driving forces in his choices, something that reaches much further than simply the decision to purchase something.

The Retail Formula©.

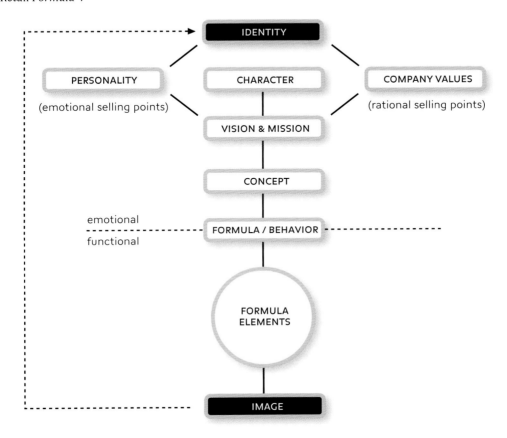

Ideally, brand identity and image are the same. In this case, the brand is perceived and valued the way it is intended to be. A company has to invest a lot of energy in order to achieve this, because all kinds of outside interferences (including the presence of and the campaigns of the competition) influence what the world sees. That changes the image that people have of a brand. For this reason, as an organization, it is important to listen to what is happening in the market and what is being said about your brand, for example, on social networks and forums. Armed with this knowledge, it is possible to actively anticipate the market and strengthen relationships with consumers. An interactive relationship with consumers is also becoming increasingly essential. In the current version of Retail 3.0, consumers primarily identify with the personality traits and emotional values of a brand. The brand becomes, as it were, a person, and the interaction a conversation. It is in this interactive and valued relationship that brand preference is created.

BUILDING THE BRAND

IN RETAIL, A BRAND IS PRIMARILY FORMED BY THE CHARACTER OF THE ORGANIZATION.

As we explained in the last chapter, the store formula is an expression of the brand, because in retail, all the aspects of the organization are visible at a single glance, because there is direct contact with the consumer. Unlike manufacturers' brands, a retail brand cannot pretend to be something other than what it is. Because the whole picture determines the image that a consumer has of a brand in a single stroke, it is necessary to know all the aspects of the organization and to have them in good order. The organization needs to know who and what it is, including its identity, its position in the market and its ambitions.

THE IDENTITY

Identity, DNA and 'it's in the genes' are all expressions that refer to brands, and they all imply deeply rooted origins for that particular brand. Identity is who you are. For people, it is often self-evident and very real, but nonetheless difficult to define or describe. Part of who we are and what we think is subconscious. Identity embraces the personality of a person, brand or organization, their standards and values (culture) and their interests (orientation). That identity is in part formed by someone's experiences, their background and history. Part of this identity is completely one's own and unique (emotional), and part of it is determined or added to by outside factors. This latter part is relatively rational and can be copied, because similar brands are all being influenced by the same things. The combination of emotional and rational elements therefore produces an inalienable and unique identity.

> *"Successful organizations distinguish themselves with a unique personality and culture that create certainty, clarity and continuity in a clear orientation that gives a sense of direction."*
>
> **RIK RIEZENBOS AND JAAP VAN DER GRINTEN IN 'POSITIONING'**

The identity is the foundation, the anchor of the organization. If it is clearly formulated, it will be a foothold for the development and the realization of the brand's activities. The identity can be translated into 'rules of behaviour' and appropriate standards and values. These are the core values of the organization. In addition, by describing the identity as a person, it makes it easier for both the organization and consumers to identify with it and even engage in the interaction. Consumers can ask themselves if that 'person' fits them or not. This can be a fictitious person, but also an existing person, whom we actually know. It is no doubt easier to imagine such a person to be someone we know. The comparison of a brand with a real person works as a good source of inspiration and a test for brand activities. One can also ask such questions as, 'What would he do in this case?', or 'Does this suit him or her?'.

Obviously, the people who work in a retail organization are determining factors in forming the brand. Their passions and their qualities are often the brand's strengths, because incorporating these into the activities of the organization motivates people. These core qualities are therefore often seen by outsiders as characteristic of the organization. In addition, the things that are happening right now and things that have happened in the past also have an influence on the brand and the prevailing organizational culture. The organization's history is its foundations and can therefore influence all the facets of its identity. It is relevant to know how an organization came about, how its founders are perceived today, whether or not there have been high and low points and what important stories are still making the rounds today. By knowing the history, one can also estimate to what degree an organization has been progressive or conservative. Is it focused on the future or are people still clinging to what happened in the past?

> *"Brand development was mainly part of the marketing department, while now it is more and more interwoven with all departments in the organisation."*
>
> **ANDY PAYNE, GLOBAL CHIEF MANAGER OF INTERBRAND**

A BRAND IS A PLATFORM, A MEETING PLACE FOR KINDRED SPIRITS.

POSITIONING IN THE MARKET

In addition to knowing who the brand is, it is important to know 'where you stand'. This determines the bandwidth in which the brand can operate and what resources can or cannot be deployed. Positioning therefore has the effect of giving direction, ensuring that activities are not just random, but that they are all grounded in the brand and will produce real results. Positioning comprises three elements: the competition, the target group and the orientation process of the organization. It is a triangular relationship between the market, the consumer and the organization.

External analysis gives insight into which market the brand finds itself in and what the competition looks like. On the basis of this, a distinctive position can be defined in regard to that competition. This distinctive position also immediately establishes the target group towards which the brand is aiming. By means of a proposition, or brand promise, this positioning can also truly be communicated to these consumers. It is important to include the orientation process here. It indicates the ways in which an organization strives to distinguish itself in the market and achieve its objectives. Is it focused on a process (production process or customer process) that is as efficient as possible, or is it centred on the customer and his needs?

In this context, Michael Treacy and Fred Wiersema have defined three so-called value strategies: operational excellence, customer intimacy and product leadership. With the first strategy, an organization strives to run a process as efficiently as possible. In this way, it can deliver products and services for a very competitive price. These organizations continually work to optimize their price/quality relationship. IKEA

pursues a policy of operational excellence, with the goal of making design as affordable as possible. IKEA also keeps its word: their Klippan sofas have become less expensive as the years pass by, because the production process continues to be improved. They also work tirelessly to make their do-it-yourself kits more efficient, thereby saving on distribution costs.

Customer intimacy involves engaging in a close relationship with customers, whereby the organization aims to continuously meet the wishes and needs of its clients. In order to get to know these customers, they engage in dialogue with them, so that they can then, on the basis of the acquired customer insight, develop new products and services, and most of all, total solutions. Thanks to this relationship, the organization can expect customers to be loyal to the brand. The Rabobank is a bank that attunes it services to its clients and develops new total solutions that apply to their needs. Within organizations like this, communications and service-oriented social skills are highly prized.

In the case of product leadership, the organization aims to deliver the best and most exceptional products in their category, in order to have advantages over their competition. The company is continuously engaged in innovation and product development. It also wants to rapidly introduce their ideas into the marketplace. Two examples of brands that follow this value strategy are Nike and Apple.

To achieve clarity in the market, for both the consumer and within the organization itself, a brand can best pursue a single value strategy. This focus ensures that consumers know what to expect from the brand, and that staff know what is and is not in line with the objectives of the organization. Activities can now be adjusted in an efficient manner, because it is clear what people are striving to achieve.

AMBITION

The third part of a brand is 'where are you headed', or in other words, the direction that is determined by the brand ambition. The ambition is the driving force of the organization and describes the organization's goals. In their book, Kus de visie wakker (Kiss the Vision Awake), Hans van der Loo, Jeroen Geelhoed and Salem Samhoud explain how 'making organizations energetic and effective' is an extremely useful way of determining this direction. According to the authors, the ambition is twofold, comprising the higher goal and the audacious goal. The first reveals the organization's reason or right to exist and refers to this as the ideals of the organization. These are deeply rooted in the organization and do not change. For that reason, this offers a firm foothold and is the guiding principle for all activities. The second ambition, the audacious goal, describes the future vision of the organization, its dream. This is what gives the activities of the organization impetus and motivation.

In the Platform Development Model©, the ambitions are formulated from the strengths of the organization, because an objective can be best achieved when the organization is good at it, when it fits the organization and everyone is behind it. In formulating the ambitions, an organization therefore always has to ask the same questions: can we do that; do we want to do that? The latter question is in fact the best indicator. This is because ambitions can best be achieved with motivation, working from core values and core qualities. At a later stage, when the vision is being formed, people will have to look at how those ambitions fit the current market and the needs of consumers, and how those ambitions can be honed and sharpened.

■ *The Value Strategies of Treacy & Wiersema.*

BRAND GUARDIANSHIP

Once there is insight into the brand, the organization and its context, the brand and its associated development strategy can be determined. The brand definition records how the brand is going to behave distinctively in the marketplace. An associated marketing strategy determines the direction the brand will take, and the trajectory it will follow in order for the brand to behave as it is intended to. Depending on the focus and the contents, a step-by-step marketing development plan can be set up. A clear framework for the brand has now been designed: who is the brand, where it stands and where it is going, as well as how it is going to get it there.

To safeguard consistency in the brand over time, in an organization where the management team regularly undergoes changes, it is advisable to involve appropriate external parties. The organization has to be able to understand the importance of this and have the courage to share responsibility with others. For consumer brands, this means a design agency and an advertising agency, because they have up-to-date knowledge of the marketplace and the consumers. In a triangular relationship between the organization, the advertising agency and the design studio, it is then possible to work on safeguarding and developing the brand. It goes without saying that a good definition of everyone's responsibilities is essential.

Brand development is a long-term process in which consistency and coherence have to be coupled to the relevant values of the brand's DNA. This is all about creating recognition and distinction in the market, establishing a clear and

■ *The triangular relationship for brand guardianship.*

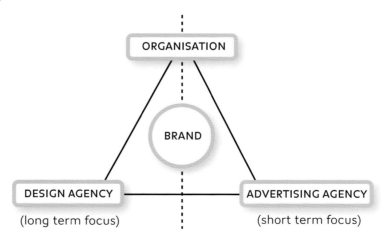

attractive position in the marketplace. Branding and design agencies have the requisite long-term strategic focus. For this reason, the role of the agencies in this set-up is to define the broad contours and framework of the brand. The brand also has to be tactical and kept close to and active in the market, with the aim of generating sales. This is the function of a communications or advertising agency, which primarily focuses on the short term. The different working methods of communications agencies and design agencies can complement one another, because each has a pace that is essential and complementary to the other. The role of the marketing manager in this triangular structure is more a role of organizing and directing the marketing communications. Thanks to this division of roles, there remains a clear focus on both the long and the short term.

IKEA shows its relevance as a brand, through its ability to reflect the way people live in every country it operates.

"An organizational culture without vision is powerless and without direction."

HANS VAN DER LOO, JEROEN GEELHOED AND SALEM SAMHOUD IN 'KISS THE VISION AWAKE'

MARKETING THE BRAND

IT IS IMPORTANT FOR AN ORGANIZATION TO KEEP IN MIND THAT THE BRAND CANNOT BE FOR EVERYONE.

If the focus is on a large target group, the brand risks being generic, its proposition unclear. This can lead to only a very few people feeling attracted to the brand. Organizations, however, often want as broad a reach as possible, because the more consumers they can appeal to, the greater their potential turnover.

DETERMINING BRAND FRAMEWORK

In order to ensure that all the activities and expressions of the brands are clear and suited to the brand and the target group, the bandwidth within which the branding takes place has to be clearly determined. What is and what is not possible is decided with the help of the brand framework. This determines the playing field and what a brand can do to retain its connection to the market. When we compare a brand personality with that of a person, we know that people manifest themselves differently in different situations. In our minds, we remain one and the same person, while the same time, we can reveal different behaviours and take on different forms, but still be convincing. There is in fact a considerable bandwidth within which we can manoeuvre. The same is true of brands. A brand can express itself differently at different times and in different situations. The brand activities have to be logical and appropriate for the brand, so that they collectively create a consistent brand image. On the other hand, there must also be space to surprise,

motivate and excite people, because it is through innovation that the relationship with consumers stays focused.

However, at a certain point, one can venture beyond this bandwidth. If someone normally does not attract special attention, dressing in dull colours, suddenly dolls themselves up in eccentric fashion, it will not look natural, and the person will not feel at ease. If the C&A clothing chain, a perfectly good store with a broad clientele, were to suddenly say that it was the hippest store in the city, people would be reluctant to accept it. Even if the clothes that they sell were to be consistent with that claim, it would not be an easy matter for them to live up to it. More importantly, their loyal customer base would be more likely to be disappointed because C&A was looking for a new group of customers.

BRAND ARCHITECTURE

If an organization wants to have a relatively diverse framework, or wants to reach extremely divergent target groups, the organization is better off selecting a brand architecture that can be developed with several brands or labels. In this way, the marketing strategy will be clear for the organization itself, as well as for the market. Wally Olins distinguishes three types of brand structures. Which of these an organization uses depends on the specific circumstances and the organization's objectives.

The first type of structure is the monolithic brand structure, in which a single brand name and a single visual identity are used for all brand activities.

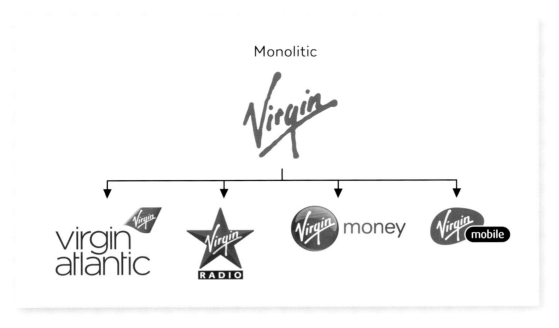

Monolitic

■ *Monolithic brand architecture according to Wally Olins.*

The brand is a quality brand and symbolizes a particular lifestyle. Because of the breadth of the brand portfolio, monolithic brands have high visibility in the marketplace. Moreover, every product or service in their portfolio makes a contribution to the visibility of the brand. Virgin is a good example of this. Its founder, Richard Branson, embodies a somewhat rebellious lifestyle, and his entrepreneurial activities have included establishing extremely diverse companies. Virgin's origins go back to the music industry, but it also includes an airline, a soft drinks producer and a provider of mobile telephony services.

A brand can express itself differently at different times and in different situations. It ensures the relationship with consumers remains surprising.

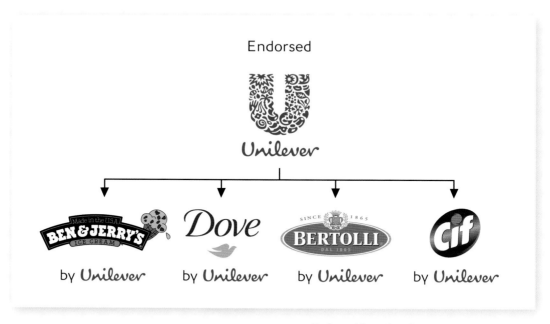

■ *Endorsed brand architecture according to Wally Olins.*

An organization can also carry different labels, all of which come together in a group. This is called endorsed branding. The name and the logo of the group are then used as the parent brand for all the brands or labels. Companies that grow by taking over other companies primarily use this form. Often, the brands they take over already have a distinct brand image and are familiar to consumers, but that brand image can be improved or better maintained. This is a standard structure in fast-moving consumer goods, the FMCG branch. Here, given the broad range of products, the name of the umbrella organization serves as the parent brand. On the other hand, such an organization also wants to demonstrate its versatility by retaining diverse product brands. For example, not so long ago, Unilever changed to endorsed branding in order to improve the visibility of the organization that stands behind its products. The

Which brand architecture fits best, depends on the ambitions of an organization and the origins of the brand.

objective here is that this visible connection will reflect positively on the products themselves.

The third variation allows the different brands to operate independently in the market, within a so-called 'branded' structure. For consumers, no interrelationships between the brands are direct-

Multi-branded

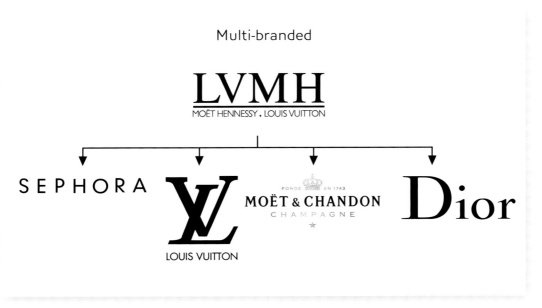

■ *Multi-branded brand architecture according to Wally Olins.*

ly evident. They experience only the consumer brand and not the organization that is behind it. Louis Vuitton Moët Hennessy, or LVMH, the parent company behind the Sephora cosmetics store formula, amongst others, is an example of this type of structure. In addition to several retail brands, they also carry diverse product brands for luxury markets. In the fashion sector, these include Donna Karan, Marc Jacobs, Louis Vuitton and Fendi. Dom Perignon and Moët & Chandon champagnes are also in their portfolio, as are Guerlain, Fendi and Dior perfumes and watches by Fred, Zenith and Dior. The advantage of carrying a portfolio with independently branded products or services is that it allows maintenance of the specific life cycle of the product. In most cases, this is not the same as that of the company. By maintaining the cycle, the product brand can develop in its own way, depending on the influen-

ces that directly affect it: the consumers and the competition. This means that it is easier to anticipate local markets. Moreover, there can be competitors amongst the other brands in the same organization's portfolio, but as long as consumers are unaware of the connection, the organization can be assured that will not have adverse effects.

In addition to these three types of brand structure, another form has also evolved: co-branding. In this case, companies engage in collaborative activities, whereby the reputations and specializations of the two brands can be united in a new product or service.

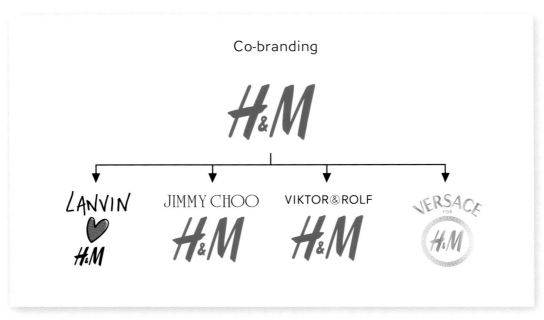

Co-branding

■ *Co-branded brand architecture according to Lisanne Bouten.*

As the name already implies, in co-branding, the names of both brands are always used. This collaboration, the joining of different forces, is the strength and the added value for consumers. There are three different types of co-branding. The first is 'symbolic co-branding', in which the second brand only adds symbolic, distinctive value to an existing product or service: the added value is in the name. One example is the Dutch lifestyle magazine, VT Wonen, which, in collaboration with a variety of licensed partners, markets products for the home, including interior accessories and furniture. The fact that these products have been selected by VT Wonen is what creates the added value. For consumers, it is a confirmation of style and good choice.

A second variation of co-branding is 'ingredient co-branding'. In this case, extra value is created by adding functions to the brands. Existing products or services are then slightly adapted or modified for the collaboration. Nike does a lot of this kind of co-branding. The knowledge that Nike has about running and about clothing and shoes suitable for sports is complemented with high-tech gadgetry from, for example, Apple and TomTom. Nike and Apple have developed Nike+ based on their understanding that music is an important and motivating factor during running. The iPod and the iPhone both include the Nike+ running programme, providing the music and recording the user's running statistics. While they are running, users can listen to encouragement from well-known sports figures. Through an online platform, running results can be saved and shared with other runners. Training programmes are also available, so that runners can share other tips and music, as well as results. Special music,

■ *Nike and the Royal Dutch Soccer Federation have collaborated on a collection.*

■ *The annual collection by H&M in collaboration with a leading designer always creates a buzz.*

put together by Nike+ users, can be downloaded via iTunes. Nike has recently combined its knowledge of running with TomTom's GPS navigation technology, so that the exact distances and speeds of a training session can be monitored, coupled with the Nike training programme.

Finally, there are the 'co-branded hybrids', in which the collaboration between two brands from different branches creates a new category. In this case, the product is always new for both the brands and the market. An example of this is the Beertender, a beer tap for home use, an alliance between Heineken and Krups. They have succeeded in making the technology and the quality of draught beer, familiar in the hotel and catering industry, available for use in the home, taking advantage of the current cocooning trend, where people are spending more time at home, entertaining their friends and family there. A second example is H&M that designs limited fashion collections in collaboration with exclusive couturiers every year.

RETAIL BRAND ARCHETYPES

THESE EXAMPLES OF SUCCESSFUL RETAILERS MAKE IT CLEAR THAT MORE THAN ONE POSITIONING IS POSSIBLE, AND THAT EVERYONE DOES THINGS IN THEIR OWN WAY. SUCCESS DEPENDS UPON A NUMBER OF FACTORS.

For example, Conran expresses a certain kind of lifestyle by linking products with his own name. But he also sells lots of brand products from brands he selects because they match his own tastes. The 'Conran figure' plays an important role in that positioning.

Sephora sells very many different brands, but also carries products under its own label. Unlike Conran, Sephora is a real store brand, but it does have a strong identity that is revealed in various ways. Sephora is innovative, is developing the perfume and personal care market and it has style.

Although Armani originally was Armani himself, the 'Armani figure' does not really play a role in the store. All products are of course sold under the Armani brand name. Although Armani's flagship store is an exception, his more 'ordinary' stores are aimed at the upper end of the market. The stores are exclusive, not just anyone walks inside (or dares to!). This is reflected in the stores' somewhat aloof and sophisticated character.

For a formula to be a success, it makes no difference whether retailers sell just their own brand, only the brands of other manufacturers, or a combination of both. Equally, it makes no difference whether retailers are at the high end of the market or are discounters. What counts is that retailers make a clear-cut choice and aim for a matching brand experience.

■ *Above: H&M is smart value.*

Below: at Uniqlo, the focus is on apparel in large volumes.

Above: in this German outdoor store, it's all about the adventure experience.

Below: colourful vegetables at Wholefoods offer the experience of lavish freshness.

In the following table we have attempted to give an overview of possible forms of retail branding. It is a mix of positioning combined with personality traits and brand values and the way in which a retailer does business. Yet this categorization does not do justice to the original and at times complex character of the wide diversity of retail brands. After all, people hate being pigeonholed too. The categories should therefore not be interpreted as a sort of 'list' from which you can simply choose a 'brand personality'. Equally, it will often be possible to place stores in more than one category (although frequently there will be one category in which they will excel). It could also turn out that this blueprint is incomplete; after all, retail is always developing.

Carin Frijters and Caroline van Beekhoff use this overview of brand archetypes in their book 'Prikkel de koopknop' (Stimulate the purchase button). Consider this a guideline and feel free to add to it.

Overview of brand archetypes in retail. ■

"The paradigm shift is that the shop will have to sell its aura rather than merely its products."

**STEPHEN ANDERSON,
RETAIL DESIGNER AT BDP**

TYPE	VARIANTIONS	EXPLANATION	RETAIL EXAMPLES
PERSONIFICATION	PRIVATE SELECTIONS	The shop reflects the character of the entrepeneur	Nicole Farhi Interior Conran shops
	THE PERSON IS THE BRAND	The founder of the company plays an important role and is definitely the concept owner	Paul Smith Tommy Hilfiger
	AN IMAGINARY PERSON IS THE BRAND	A fictitious person is presented as frontman.	Colette, Trader Joe's, Ted Baker
SOCIALLY RESPONSIBLE ENTREPENEURSHIP (SRE)	ENVIRONMENT ORIENTED	SRE from an environmental and ideological standpoint	Bodyshop, Aveda
	CRITICAL OF SOCIAL STRUCTURE	Social issues/facts exposed/shown in different light	Benetton
DISCOUNT	SUPER DISCOUNT	It's only about price	Action, Target, Aldi, Primark
SMART VALUE	SMART AND GOOD BUY FOR A GREAT PRICE	Price is important, but added value is created through the manifestation of wilfullness and style	Muji, Hema, H&M
INNOVATIVE	VERY SPECIFIQUE AND UNIQUE	The unique, experimental design of the store plays a very important role in the proposition	Comme des Garçons, Prada
	MARKET LEADER	A forerunner in terms of new developments	Apple, Nespresso
AUTHENTICITY	TRADITIONAL, NOSTALGIC	Old values/times revived, or freshly transformed into the spirit of the times	Burberry, Mont Blanc
	STORYTELLING	A sincere story has to convince the customer	Antropology, Trader Joe's
	SINCERE, RELIABLE	It's important that the consumer trusts you (mostly services)	Triodos Bank, Apple
SOPHISTICATED	UPPER CLASS	In a rather aloof manner	Gucci, Armani, Tiffany's
	THE STORE AS A STAGE	Focus on experience and lifestyle	Hermès, Prada, Merci
EXPERIENCE	TOTAL IMMERSION	The experience is very explicit and involves consumers	Nike Town, Disney Store, American Girl Place, Desigual
	MULTI-SENSORY	An experience in a more implicit, emotional or spiritual level	Rituals, Lush, Sephora, Cosmetic Garden
RUGGEDNESS	TOUGH, OUTDOOSY	Challenging experience, focusing on activities	The North Face, Patagonia
	MANLY	Focus on men's hobbies, such as do-it-yourself jobs	MediaMarkt, Hornbach, Gamma
TRENDY	CONTEMPORARY	Retail trends made accessible through appearance and assortment	Mango, Zara, Abercrombie & Fitch, Hollister, IKEA
	HIP, TRENDSETTING	Retail are trendsetting through appearance and assortment, and often focus on a specific, fashionable audience	Diesel, Gstar, Urban Outfitters, TopShop
ABUNDANCE	LITERALLY	Large volumes the product does the job	Uniqlo, Dean&Deluca, MediaMarkt
	FIGURATIVELY	The product plays a part in creating the atmosphere	IKEA, Barnes and Noble, Eataly, WholeFoods

8.
DESIGNING THE FORMULA

Bringing the brand to life

ABOUT BUILDING THE PLATFORM FOR BRAND AND CONSUMER,
THE CENTRAL ROLE OF THE CONSUMER, THE DESIGN PROCESS BASED ON
THREE PILLARS©, THE NEED FOR COOPERATION BETWEEN ALL STAKE-
HOLDERS, THE IMPORTANCE OF CONTINUOUS DEVELOPMENT AND
THE LAYERING OF STORE COMMUNICATION.

1+1=1

The secret concept for integrated formula development

The Nespresso boutique in Paris attracts curiosity in the period before it was opened.

THE LAST CHAPTER WAS ABOUT DEVELO-PING A RETAIL BRAND, WHICH FORMS THE BASIS FOR THE RETAIL FORMULA AND ITS DEVELOPMENT. WHEN YOU HAVE DEFINED YOUR BRAND, IT IS TIME TO BRING IT TO LIFE, TO LAUNCH IT ONTO THE MARKET AND INTO THE MINDS OF CONSUMERS.

As explained earlier and shown in the Platform Development Model©, a retail formula is a perfect platform to showcase all aspects of the brand and enable it to interact with consumers.

However, this platform is bigger than the physical store alone; the retail formula also consists of the virtual store, the website, any retail formats and ultimately every single component of the model. This chapter looks at the development and design of these retail elements, which come together to form the store formula and brand image.

Design gives form to the thought: formula development is therefore not about creating an attractive blend of modern colours and materials. Ultimately, retail design is a unique expression of the brand and its ambitions. For existing store

formulas, this is often a process of continuing development, an optimization of the formula. In that case, all the existing store components need to be re-examined: It may be necessary to incorporate new aspects and omit others that are no longer relevant. This container, with its functions and components, is reassembled in a new contemporary design. In the heated process of market identity definition and its translation into a new retail concept, it is important always to keep the consumer in mind. Ultimately it will be the consumer that will need to feel drawn to the whole proposition, the trinity that makes up the brand: its identity, its market position and its ambition. The symbiosis between the consumer and the company will be partly responsible for the formula's success.

Retail design is a unique expression of the brand and its ambitions.

Consumers base their choice of store on a combination of what is on offer, who is offering it and how it is offered: this is the secret of the retail concept. It is not so much about the assortment on offer, since unique products are rare and successful products rarely stay that way. Offering products in the specific context can make them unique. This context can be created by asking yourself what the products can mean for the consumer, both rationally and emotionally. This meaning may be based on the way the consumer buys or uses the product, on a link to a lifestyle or an unexpected combination of products. This, combined with who you are, your unique identity, is what makes the difference and creates the added value. By translating these insights into retail design, you create a link with your target consumer who will then choose your store.

154

"It is by innovating that brands remain relevant, justify their price premium and confirm their status as points of reference. Innovation is the lifeblood of a brand."

JEAN-NOEL KAPFERER

THE DESIGN PROCESS

IDEALLY, THE DEVELOPMENT OF THE RETAIL FORMULA WILL OCCUR IN CLOSE COOPERATION BETWEEN THE RETAIL ORGANIZATION AND DESIGN AGENCY.

The practical knowledge and experience of modern stores provides valuable information for the design process, because rather than being a showroom, the store needs to be a successful retail environment that transforms lookers into buyers. A second reason why it is important for the retail organization to be closely involved in the process of design is the need for internal support: because it is ultimately their store, they need to feel at home in it and to be able to identify with the decisions made during the design process. This support can be used to create enthusiasm across the rest of the organization. As mentioned earlier, the Platform Development Model© is both a development and a launch platform. It provides support both before and during the process of retail formula design; but even when the store has been fully realized, all the retail elements need to be in order. This is a major challenge for the organization: staff need to be well-trained and to stay fully motivated. Visual merchandising needs to be stylish and eye-catching, so that it continues to provide inspiration and furnishings need to stay looking good and be replaced or repaired if damaged. Of course, it is also essential for the operational parts of the store, such as distribution, to be in order, to ensure that the shelves stay stocked. If the retail organization understands the formula properly, it will be easier for them to organize and maintain the formula.

The process of formula development starts from a broad base: a range of options and possibilities are examined in the early stages, which ultimately result in choices being made. As the process progresses, the picture gradually becomes more concrete. In the design process, it is important not to allow yourself to be inhibited by all sorts of practical considerations too soon, despite the fact that retailers have a tendency to apply all their experiences on the retail floor in the early stages of the process. As outlined earlier, this experience is important information but it must not be allowed to obstruct innovation and creativity. In order to prevent branding, creativity and practical considerations from getting in each other's way, the Three Pillars© has been developed. In the development process, each pillar has its own position, its own associated approach and its own solution.

THE FIRST PILLAR: BRAND IMAGE

The first pillar concerns the brand identity, and from the market perspective, the brand image. This is a strategic long-term process. It involves an extensive assessment of the company's identity, positioning and ambition. This is recorded in the brand definition and visualization, which form the basis for all brand communications and activities and therefore also for the formula development. How innovative will the store be and how will the consumer's needs be catered for throughout the entire customer journey? This also involves the various channels and formats. How will the store concept operate and how will it manifest itself visually and more importantly differently? The answers to these questions can be found by exploring different scenarios: visualizations of the store as a meeting place for the brand and the customer. Each scenario can focus on one of the elements of the brand definition and the customer relationship: in other words the added value of the brand. In this, it is all about identifying the right perspective or perspectives in order to enthuse and inspire the core customer and the related, new customer groups, so they

■ *The Three Pillars©.*

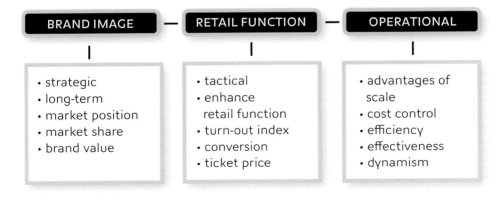

will visit the store more often and spend more. Actually configuring the brand is achieved by means of a combination of tangible, visual and intangible values, which ultimately take shape as tangible elements, with their own style, tone of voice and look & feel. This translation of the brand will then manifest itself in the market share and brand value.

The Three Pillars© makes the integrated development process transparent and manageable.

By choosing one of the potential scenarios, a decision will be made on the extent to which the formula development will be evolutionary or revolutionary. This will then be compiled into a concept: the basis for formula development. It will include statements about all of the retail elements. Firstly, mood boards can be used to create an impression of the intended store image, both in terms of its look & feel and the tone of voice of in-store communications. References can also be given for possible product presentations, visual merchandising, inspiration and information points, the use of materials and colour. Part of the concept can also include an assessment of how customer service might take shape: for example, in the role played by staff or in digital solutions and in-store communication. This could include silent salesmen, self-scanning facilities, apps that provide additional information on the sales floor, in-store access to the webshop, a virtual personal shopper and much more. The service concept reveals a lot about how progressive the brand is,

but most importantly it puts the customer first. It is all about making the very best of what the store has to offer.

It is also possible to translate the intended store image and proposition into a draft layout. What route will the customer take through the store? How will routing be used to ensure the customer passes through the entire store and how will the various aspects of the brand be most effectively communicated? Layout is a major, decisive factor in customer convenience and their behaviour.

In the development of the Dutch convenience supermarket AH toGo, the layout was based on two types of target customers. The first of these are people out and about who want to pick up some food or drink for the train, for example. The second group of target customers includes those on their way home who want to do their shopping there so they will not need to go to a regular supermarket. They are looking for a meal to cook or heat up at home, a bottle of wine or something practical that they may have forgotten. Both types of customer have a different pace and mindset: one is in a hurry to catch the train, the other is more relaxed as they head home. These two different paces are reflected in the store. At the front, there is a fast lane, guiding the customer past the fresh sandwiches and coffee and then directly to the checkout. But there is also a slow lane, directing the customer to the rear of the store, where they have more time to search among the assortment at their convenience. The hurried and relaxed customers do not get in each other's way because they are routed more or less separately through the store.

Another example can be seen in the new store concept launched by Pearle Opticians in the

Netherlands at the end of 2010. Pearle Opticians positions itself in the middle of the market and distinguishes itself from low-cost players by means of its service and quality. Its other competitors are more expensive, independent opticians. Pearle distinguishes itself from them by offering a wide assortment at an affordable price. The key points of service, quality and an extensive assortment at a good price are therefore made visible by more or less literally showcasing them in the store. This is expressed in a service section and a browsing section, which provides an overview of the assortment. This division is made visible through the store experience and the floor and ceiling finishing.

■ *Even outside the shop, the fast and longer route in the Dutch convenience store AH toGo are visible.*

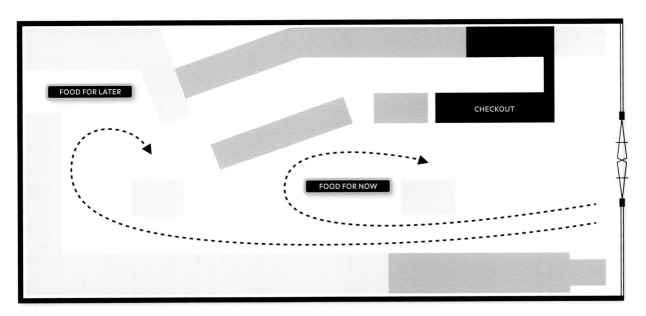

FOOD FOR LATER

CHECKOUT

FOOD FOR NOW

■ *The layout shows that you can shop at two tempos in AH toGo.*

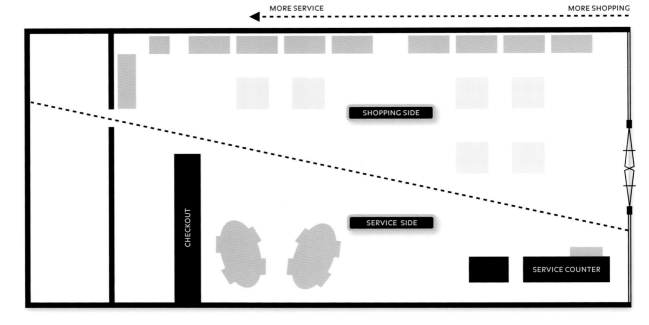

MORE SERVICE ← - MORE SHOPPING

SHOPPING SIDE

SERVICE SIDE

CHECKOUT

SERVICE COUNTER

Pearle Opticians stores in the Netherlands distinguish between service and assortment. Up front, the emphasis is on shopping, to tempt the customer into the store, while further back the focus shifts to personal attention, reflecting the customer journey.

By including a statement about all the aspects of the formula in the concept, you can create a solid basis for the future store formula. The concept visualizes the dream, the thought that needs to be given form. In the further process, this first pillar serves as a means of assessing whether what is developed still reflects this concept.

THE SECOND PILLAR: RETAIL FUNCTION

The second pillar involves the store function process and is technical in nature. When we consider the physical store, we need to address such issues as: how does the store work, what is the entrance like, the routing, the assortment group allocation plan, the structure within the departments, sight

lines, product presentation, lighting (often underestimated, especially in changing rooms!), in-store communication and overall design, as well as the back-end of the store (logistical processes, staff rooms, etc.)? Retail design can provide the answers to these questions. Together, the gestalt of all these aspects will create the store experience and have an impact on the brand experience. Even for the virtual store, there are similar questions that need to be answered through design: how do you enter (the homepage or start page), how do you navigate through the site and is communication clear? And, of course, the physical and virtual stores of any brand will need to be connected and reinforce each other and recognizably originate from the same source.

A key characteristic of retail design is its combination of aesthetics and function, or how it looks and how it works. The first purpose of this function is to attract consumers into the store (or webshop). After that, you want to keep them in the store by achieving a smooth flow within and between the departments, through inspirational product presentations and a pleasant atmosphere. To achieve this, all the retail elements need to be designed on the basis of the concept and the intended brand image. The aim is to seduce the customer into buying: how can he be inspired and above all seduced to make impulse purchases? What logical assortment clusters are there and how can you create space for cross-selling? What layout will ensure that the customer passes through the entire store? In a supermarket, the vegetables and fruit are often presented first in order to give an attractive, high-quality and fresh impression. This impression sets the tone for the whole store. Sometimes, bread and milk are placed towards the back of the store, because customers come specifically looking for them and can therefore be compelled to go to the back of the store.

"Man is the measure of all things."

PROTAGORAS

When it comes to what the retailer can do for the customer, inspiration is the keyword. In that respect, you should always give more than customers expect: more service, a novel idea or a special/original promotion (which need not necessarily focus on price) and make it easy for them. This kind of inspirational environment and an effectively regulated customer flow can do wonders for conversion and ticket price levels. In order to ensure that the store remains inspirational, you will need to renew or refresh the store image from time to time. This surprises

consumers. As the world moves faster and we are confronted with so many different things on a daily basis, it is increasingly difficult to make an impression. Leaving retail design unchanged for as long as seven years is not a very good idea. Even if a number of key elements are changed from time to time (while, of course, maintaining a balanced Platform Development©!), it is possible to create a varied store image which continues to attract customers inside.

Communication is also an important part of an inspirational formula. In order to communicate the proposition and added value, the brand will need to speak to the customer: literally and figuratively, instrumentally and aspirationally. Communication is part of the process in which a store brand develops a relationship with the consumer. In developing layered in-store communication, it is important to keep in mind the different consecutive phases of the customer journey. At each point in this process – at home, out and about, on the internet (mobile or otherwise) and at different places in the store – you must take account of the customer mindset at that time. For the store itself, this means an attractive store frontage that draws customers' attention, navigation through the store, appropriate decor, inspiration, information, promotional communication, as well as pricing and product information at shelf level. Primarily, this is about attracting customers' attention with a view to drawing them into the store or webshop and then highlighting the product range and special offers. The closer the customer comes to potential seduction and the purchase, the more focused the information must be. This is where the human aspect takes precedence: all communications must be designed in proportion to the customer's perspective. For physical retail, the front of the store in the high street needs to be writ large and scream out to customers. When entering the store, navigation needs to be legible, visible and clear. But ultimately, product communication needs to adopt a format that is relevant and visible to someone standing next to it. In other words: man is the measure of all things

The key is therefore to ensure you achieve attraction in order to enable a transaction to take place. Although it has long been a fixture in major stores, the escalator was actually the first major example of the effective generation of customer flow. It suddenly provided easy access to the upper stories, with amazing consequences for the ticket price. People stayed longer, saw more and bought more.

In developing new solutions for communication, routing, departmental structure and product presentation, visual retail design will always need to adapt to the organization's renewed or updated vigour. The options and freedoms available to retail designers vary from retailer to retailer: for small stores they are very different than for major stores and they are different again for discounters or specialist outlets.

THE THIRD PILLAR: OPERATIONAL

The third pillar concerns the operational process of implementation, as well as everyday dealings with the store. This technical aspect must be taken account of in retail design. Ultimately, it is all about feasibility, advantages of scale, modularity, flexibility, cost control and maintenance. It involves material knowledge of durability and cost price, knowledge about systems, about construction projects and the processes associated with them. Alongside this, is the everyday dynamism of the

When the escalator was introduced, revenue showed a massive growth.

store: variation and change, flexibility and impulse generation. If the initial fixed resource costs were low, part of the budget could be used for variable elements to enable flexibility over the years. This enables the store formula to continually adapt to the market, to customer needs and the spirit of the age. The result is a modular and dynamic store that never fails to surprise the consumer. How exactly it should be configured will in part depend on the sector, because obviously a car tyre specialist will have a lower visit frequency level than a department store. Logically, the former will need to adapt less and focus less on impulse purchases, though it will still need to do both these things. In this case, module design, types of presentation and, of course, in-store communications are the most important aspects. Often, these aspects have a short life and the materials and production methods may therefore need to reflect this. This is an obligation in terms of operational costs and the environment.

FIRST PILLAR

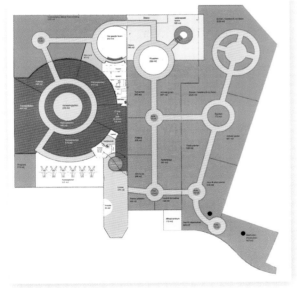

SECOND PILLAR

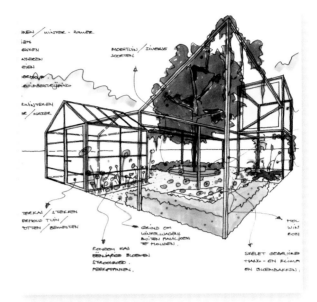

■ The first pillar of Dutch garden centre Intratuin is about the visual identity and the layout of the store. This answers the questions: 'How can the brand be recognized and how will the customer be served?'

■ As part of the second pillar, the functional design is shaped and layout developed into a shelving plan.

In the third pillar, the design is realized and made operational. Then the result can be truly admired.

"One of our core philo-sophies is that we spend the money that other companies spend on marke-ting to create a store experience that exceeds people's expectations. We don't spend money on messages, we invest in execution."

**GLEN SENK,
PRESIDENT VAN ANTHROPOLOGY**

A CONTINUOUS PROCESS

THE THREE PILLARS© MODEL AND THE PLATFORM DEVELOPMENT MODEL© ARE CLOSELY INTERRELATED.

The Three Pillars© and the Platform Development Model© are closely interrelated. The three pillars of the first model are all of a different order, but form an indivisible unit. Experience shows that it is necessary to approach these pillars both separately and in combination. Separately, because they are of a different order and consistency and therefore need to be developed with a specialist approach and with full attention. In combination, because the links between the elements form the holistic whole. They are therefore so closely interrelated that they are all equally important and if they are to form a strong basis, all three need to be of corresponding quality and equal magnitude. In this, this model reflects the basic principles of the Platform Development Model©.

Equally, the Platform Development Model© is also a source of information that is necessary for the Three Pillars© and vice-versa. Knowledge of the brand context, the roots of the formula, can be obtained from the Platform Development Model©, providing input for the first pillar. The retail elements required for the formula, the understanding of the extent to which they have been developed and require further development, emerge from the Platform Development Model©, but are then operationalized as part of the second pillar. And the third pillar makes it possible for the store formula actually to be realized and to continue to function in the longer term.

The interaction between both models remains an issue because it will continue to be necessary to anticipate and respond to the changing context of the formula. This is part of a retailer's make-up. Retailers have always been people of the here and now, since they will always respond immediately to market conditions. However, most successful retail formulas are young and many of the old ones have disappeared, because although they may have responded immediately to the market, they demonstrated little strategic vision. This strategic vision can primarily be found in the first pillar, which examines personality and how it can be developed as well as contemporary relevance for the market and employees (and to a lesser extent for the direct needs of shareholders). With this pillar to provide continuous direction, a store formula would never need to stop developing. By taking small steps, by evolving and taking major strides where necessary. By responding to short-term influences, but never losing sight of the long-term focus.

Things have to look simple and be simple - for the customer, at least. But there is no simple way to achieve that; you have to go through it all.

IN-STORE COMMUNICATION

IN-STORE COMMUNICATION PROVIDES AN EXTREMELY IMPORTANT SUPPORT FOR CUSTOMER FLOW. IT IS THE MEANS OF ACCOMPANYING THE CUSTOMER ON THE JOURNEY FROM THE SOFA AT HOME TO THE ULTIMATE PURCHASE

164

Whether it's physical, virtual or otherwise. For each step, appropriate images, resources and impulses need to be designed that reflect the personality of the brand and link together each of these steps. Four key areas of focus apply to this (disregarding the staff, strictly speaking):

- Focus on formula and brand
- Focus on function
- Focus on product
- Focus on promotion

I. FOCUS ON FORMULA AND BRAND

This includes all literal and figurative communications that relate to the formula and the brand. It might be a statement at the entrance, with promises for the customer. It could be the store name and logo that reappear throughout the store. Communication that focuses on formula and brand increases the likelihood that the customer will remember the brand name, ensuring it remains or becomes top-of-mind. However, more intangible means will also be needed in order to convey the actual brand personality. After all, it is not possible to communicate or convey this personality literally: people need to experience it, through their senses (through music, smells, lighting, choice of materials, the stimulation of taste, etc.). Two- and three-dimensional elements support the whole, contributing to the atmosphere, the tone & style. Graphic resources include typography, colour, pictograms and images (photography, digital and moving images) and three-dimensional resources include elements such as design, visual merchandising (volume, lifestyle, product combinations, etc.), the layout, design and routing of the store, as well as intangible aspects such as smell, music or light. All of these elements combined (multisensory experiences) convey the store personality and form the store experience.

The illustrations show examples of stores that have created their own characteristic store atmosphere.

In addition to the store brand, the sector and type of store also determine the tone & style. Obviously, the atmosphere in a discount store will be different from that at a specialist and a brown and white goods store will feel different from a jeweller's. Just compare the two supermarkets shown in the photographs.

■ l. In the early stages of the customer journey, the retailer wants to confirm to the consumer that they are on the right path. Outside its stores, Boots highlights the product categories it has inside (left), and people at London's Luton airport are encouraged to find their way to the shopping area (right).

■ l. On the move, a consumer comes into contact with brand-oriented communication, such as the Marks & Spencer poster (top left) or the Abercrombie & Fitch advertisement on the bus (right), both in London. The aim is to convey the emotion and atmosphere of the brand.

■ **I.** *The exterior of the shop tells potential customers what they can expect inside. In the case of the Smoke Shop, it is very literal (top left), and Apple adopts a direct approach (centre left).*

In the shop there is the opportunity to make a bold statement about what the brand stands for, focusing on the product, for example, as Pret-a-Manger does (left) or on the history of the company, like Heal's (right).

II. FOCUS ON FUNCTION

In-store communication includes functional elements such as the signs directing customers around the stores, departmental signs and signs for services. Signs are used to clarify the layout and routing through the store for the customer. Depending on the size of the store, maps may be needed or departmental name signs may suffice. The illustrations here provide a few examples of highly unusual types of functional signing: they show that it is possible to express your personality in something as mundane as directions.

The routine, layout and structure of the store also help ensure that someone can find their way within the store easily or not so easily. Obviously, the routing, layout and structure of the store must be based on logic. In smaller stores, the focus will be more on the layout and structure of the store space, whereas routing will play a more important role in department stores and other major stores. Sometimes, routing can be rigorously and strictly enforced whereas in other stores you may be free to move around as and where you wish. For example, IKEA has a very fixed route, passing through all the departments, which is difficult to avoid, unless you know the shortcuts. But the problem with these types of shortcuts is that you do not know what departments you are missing. The consumer needs to have an overview in order to be able to make well-considered choices to do or not do something.

II. *Functional in-store communication highlights the departments (Heal's top, centre Barnes & Noble) or shows store layout (John Lewis Partnership).*

children's floor
bedlinen
blankets
toys
accessories
furniture

lower ground floor
dining furniture
tableware
glassware
table linen
cushions
lighting
rugs
stationery
vases

III. FOCUS ON PRODUCT

The aim is for the customer to be able, without assistance, to find out as much as possible about the products and product groups. In that respect, information that is focused on products can largely replace the staff. In this, it is important that the information is effective and includes the price. It must also be presented in such a way that it enables the customer to compare the product features and make an effective choice. This layer of communication can also be used to inspire the customer, for example by focusing on the brand atmosphere of the product within the store environment. In supermarkets, this is often done by placing products from the same manufacturer alongside each other, creating interplay between the packaging. Other examples include store window displays, visual merchandising and shop-in-shop set-ups. Mobile social media can provide additional support and offer added value, for example by enabling access to product reviews by previous purchasers or showing an aspirational brand or product video. Communication focused on products also offers the opportunity to tell the customer the story behind the product's origin or how it is manufactured. It is important that this information supports the brand personality, because consistency and authenticity are vital in retail branding.

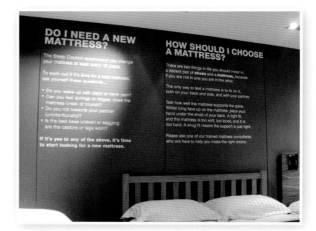

■ *III. Product-oriented communication helps people to make a choice. Computers can be helpful (Selfridges above), but Heal's assists by asking some honest questions (below).*

Richt page: a simple but effective aid in Muji stores shows which size you need (top left). A guide to the fabrics in Uniqlo's clothing explains the benefits for users (centre left) and the label in a garment shows that it's Saks Fifth Avenue's private label.

Communication alongside the product shows the product combination (Muji right). The display highlights the best wine and meal combinations (centre right). A form of product branding: Trader Joe's own brand of Mexican beer is aptly named Trader Jose (bottom right).

169

IV. FOCUS ON PROMOTIONS

Often this is a highly present layer of in-store communication, seen in many stores. Especially when supply increases, competition between comparable products in stores will grow. Offering the lowest price and special offers is a commonly-used strategy for attracting consumers.

Promotions can be communicated at store level, departmental level or product level. At store level, the promotion can be linked to a theme, which can be a more pleasant way of providing offers than major price cuts. Compare the promotional options for manufacturing brands: they are generally limited to new product launches and the promotion of new varieties or a simple 3-for-the-price-of-2 offer. For a store, it is easier to capitalize on seasons or special holidays or to develop a unique, possibly annual theme. On such occasions, a store can truly exploit its personality: by doing something outrageous, something exciting, something unexpected. It can look completely different for a short period, whilst ensuring the change fits in with the store personality. This kind of store theme can also be used for a standard clear-out sale, adding to its value. An excellent example of this is the 'Three Crazy Days' ('Drie Dwaze Dagen') promotion at De Bijenkorf, a Dutch department store that targets the upper market segment. For three days, the whole store is bright yellow and packed with crazy offers everywhere. But the store retains its familiar personality and reputation, even though it may have some different customers (bargain-hunters).

■ Left page: the 'Three Crazy Days' campaign is pre-announced outside and inside there is total immersion at Dutch department store De Bijenkorf.

This page: promotions do not have to be about price alone: they can provide the final impetus to buy, as in TopShop (top left). Or highlight the benefits of using the product (Superdrug, top right). Bulk volumes also boost sales. The advantages of bulk-buying are showcased here by Vomar Voordeelmarkt (centre left) and Wholefoods (centre right). Jumbo sends a message to departing customers to encourage them to return (bottom right).

9.
THE CUSTOMER JOURNEY

The path from need to purchase

ABOUT THE CONTINUOUS CHAIN OF CONTACTS, THE DEVELOPMENT FROM
A LINEAR TO A VARIED AND DYNAMIC PROCESS, THE CHANGING MINDSETS
OF CONSUMERS, THEIR PURCHASING PROCESS AND HOW TO ADAPT TO IT
AS A RETAILER, ABOUT THE NEED FOR AN OMNI-CHANNEL STRATEGY AND
INFLUENCING SHOPPING BEHAVIOUR.

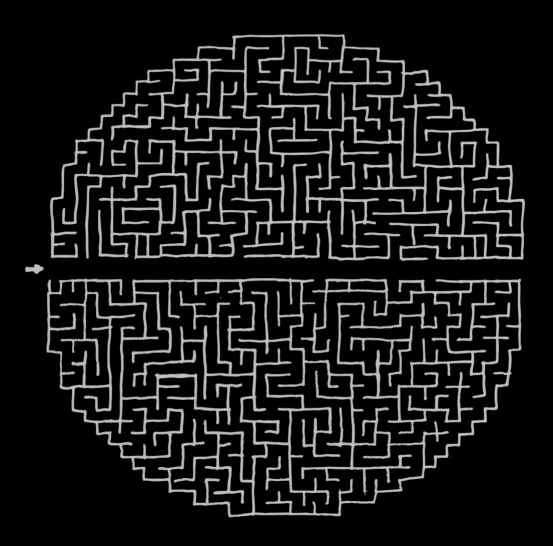

THE RIGHT WAY

The retailer would prefer that the consumer comes straight to his product

■ *The customer journey is the route to the store. At Abercrombie & Fitch that means standing in line outside, as this picture of the Paris branch shows.*

IN THE PLATFORM DEVELOPMENT MODEL©, THE RETAIL CHOICE DIAGRAM© IS THE FACTOR THAT BRINGS THE RETAIL FORMULA AND ITS CONTEXT TOGETHER.

In the model, this contact is visualized through the interface between the external side, the outside world and people, and the internal side, from the brand essence to the store concept. This layer covers all the stages that the customer must pass through and all the choices he faces from the first introduction to the brand through to the purchase of a product in a physical or virtual store. This customer journey is an essential part of the retail process and an important factor in the formula's success. The retailer needs to guide the consumer through this process, providing assistance in making choices and continually seducing the consumer to approach the formula, enter it and proceed to make a purchase. This therefore needs to be a consecutive chain in order to ensure that the retailer and consumer are linked together: a commitment that becomes closer and more personal as the customer journey progresses. To achieve this, the retailer must communicate a relevant message at every point in order to ensure that the consumer's enthusiasm does not fade. The aim is for the consumer to become a customer. This is no easy challenge, because unexpected scenarios can easily put paid to planned visits to the store: another retailer may suddenly attract the consumer's attention, moaning children may distract them, or an offer may make them change their mind.

During the customer journey the retailer should guide the customer, providing assistance in making choices and continually seducing the consumer to the store and proceed to make a purchase.

The customer journey has now become enormously complicated and multifaceted and has developed into an omni-channel process. In the past, the offering was less varied, which meant that the customer journey was a simpler, more direct process from the sofa at home to the ultimate purchase. In those days, it was the TV ad or free press that provided the trigger to go to the store to buy a particular product or offer.

Nowadays, the consumer faces various options and choices in different places and a variety of media to provide information and help make the ultimate purchase. This change to the customer journey is partly because the consumer has become more complex: he has changing needs and behaves differently depending on the particular situation. If a retailer is to be relevant in all of these different situations, the message needs to be flexible and the points of contact varied. On the other hand, the possibilities offered by the digital world are also responsible for this shift: the enormous success of smartphones in particular means that consumers no longer only have access to the internet at home, but anywhere and at any time. Even when they are out and about and in the store. What's more, several different types of media are increasingly being used simultaneously in the purchasing process. Customers get the information they need in the store, on the website, in the leaflet or from reviews via social media. This means that he is well-informed of the options available. This has led to changes in the traditional process of orientation within the physical store as well as the process of purchasing. The consumer arrives at the store fully prepared and armed with knowledge and is even able to obtain additional information via mobile internet at any time, in order to make a focused and targeted purchase. But the process also works the other way around: staff in the store can be approached for advice and the customer then consults the internet to find the best price and to buy the product online. This is particularly the case when people buy consumer durables, but it applies equally to booking holidays. These are also the sectors that face a fight for survival if they do not quickly adapt to this increasingly dynamic customer journey. Thanks to the use of multimedia, the internet is no longer simply an alternative to the physical store. It has become complementary: the options offered by fixed and mobile internet are like an additional layer on top of physical retail. Augmented reality, QR codes and apps are the tools available today to provide additional information and possibilities for special offers and purchases. Developments in this area are moving extremely rapidly and are probably still in their very early stages.

"The sender/receiver model has made way for a dialogue, in which the customer finds his or her own way. Companies should think themselves lucky if they are part of their customer journey."

BEATE VAN DONGEN, PARTNER VODW MARKETING

THE PROCESS OF RETAIL CHOICE

ALTHOUGH THE CUSTOMER JOURNEY NEED NO LONGER INVOLVE A PHYSICAL VISIT TO THE STORE – SIMPLY BECAUSE IT IS NO LONGER NECESSARY TO GO THERE IN ORDER TO BUY SOMETHING – PEOPLE'S OPTIONS AND CHOICES REMAIN AND THESE STILL PLAY A ROLE IN THE DIFFE-RENT PHASES OF THE PURCHASING PROCESS.

Nevertheless, these technical developments do provide new possibilities that accentuate and facilitate specific behaviour and actions. In most cases, this means that the route towards the ultimate purchase becomes more varied.

This purchasing process and the various choices are shown in the Retail Choice Diagram©. By making specific choices at every stage, the consumer gradually progresses through the purchasing process and at every stage his mindset changes and there are shifts in focus and interest. In their white paper, entitled 'Shopper vs. Consumer: Communicating to Shifting Mindsets', the Integer

Group sites four different mindsets: 'awareness', 'consideration', 'intent' and 'purchase'. In the phase leading up to a purchase, the consumer becomes aware of a brand and its offering. He then considers whether to make a potential purchase. During the 'awareness' and 'consideration' mindsets, the retailer must actively seek out contact with the consumer in order to seduce him or her to enter the store. This means that the retailer needs to be where the consumer is at that moment: whether it's at home, out and about or on the internet. If the consumer is successfully seduced, the purchasing consideration is converted into an intention to buy. The consumer becomes a shopper. At this stage, the retailer must converse with him or her at an individual level in order to convince the shopper personally to proceed to a purchase. Even after the purchase, it is important to ensure the customer remains connected to the brand, with the aim of enticing him or her to make another purchase.

If aware of these different mindsets, the retailer can anticipate them, provide assistance in making

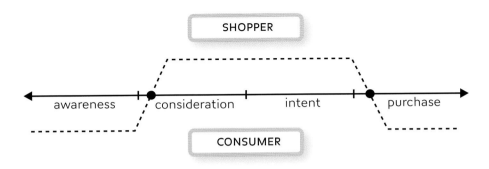

During the customer journey people alternate their roles as consumers and shoppers, depending on their changing mindsets, according to The Integer Group.

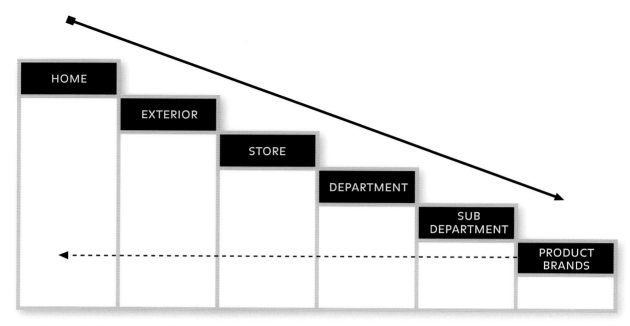

■ *The Retail Choice Diagram©.*

choices where possible and above all develop the relationship as the journey progresses. At all relevant points in the retail choice process, the retailer must be present and must have an interesting proposition for the consumer. The right time, the right place, the right proposition: ensure that you are top-of-mind as a retailer and stay there for your consumers. It is no easy task becoming number one, and even more difficult staying there. What a retailer can do is ensure that all the steps that the consumer makes are catered for: from the sofa at home to the product on the shelf. The Retail Choice Diagram© illustrates this: on the one hand it highlights the physical steps and mental choices that the customer actually needs to go through in order to buy a random product. On the other hand, it shows the resources that the retailer has at his disposal in guiding the customer at each of these steps.

THE RETAIL CHOICE DIAGRAM© FROM THE CUSTOMER'S PERSPECTIVE

THE RETAIL CHOICE DIAGRAM© STARTS WHEN THE CONSUMER HAS A SPECIFIC NEED OR A NEED IS TRIGGERED BY SEEING OR EXPERIENCING A BRAND OR PRODUCT.

Because, by their nature, people are always looking for the best, the quest to fulfil this identified need as effectively as possible will now begin. Since we are confronted by multiple impressions simultaneously in the high street or on the internet, the retail choice process is strongly based on interpretation and on the pre-existing knowledge that we all have. The consumer will use this to compile a shortlist of potential brands. Part of this will consist of stores that are already familiar, but, depending on the type of purchase, he may also wish to explore further and consider other options. To do this, knowledge can be obtained through the traditional channels, such as advertising on TV, radio and in magazines, leaflets and billboards. Although there are signs that the influence of these types of media is beginning to decline, they remain for many people a tried-and-trusted way of obtaining information and they also continue to reach large groups of people. Moreover, the internet has significantly increased the potential to explore. The whole world's offering is suddenly within reach. Because retail is a social activity, the consumer will also involve other people to help filter these worldwide options: he will ask friends, family and acquaintances to confirm or improve the planned purchase. After all, the opinion of like-minded people will help to identify how best to meet the need. This is nothing new: consumers have always listened to other people's recommendations. But the social reach has become much larger, more efficient and relevant thanks to the options offered by the internet and social media. Various online forums are available to discuss potential purchases. Based on one's own preferences and frame of reference, a number of brands can then be selected. This interaction has significantly increased the power of the consumer. Someone who is a complete stranger, but nevertheless like-minded, can advise against the planned purchase. If argued well, this advice may be followed. In that respect, consumers trust each other more than they trust the retailer: experience is rated more highly than the knowledge and advice of a specialist. The quality of recommendations is also improving, since people are increasingly concerned about their online reputation and therefore aim to ensure the opinion they give is a valuable one. Rapid developments in smartphone technology also mean that reviews can even be done in real-time, making them even more relevant. But this also makes it more difficult for retailers to monitor the customer journey. This is why it is all the more important that there are valuable points of contact with the consumer during the various phases of the purchasing process.

Specific details are provided with the cheese at Wholefoods.

■ *Lush really plays on the senses, through the scent of the soap and the visual merchandising.*

■ *A 'sound shower' gives the customer a personal experience.*

180

Based on the shortlist compiled, the consumer will then set off, with an image of a real or notional high street in mind. He will imagine the stores to visit and in what sequence. This also applies to online stores: people start by imagining in their mind's eye what the website looks like and what steps will be needed to reach it, as well as other websites he might also want to visit. If the shopping is based on an actual need, more rational considerations will determine the shops that are shortlisted in the mind. In that case, location will be an important consideration, as well as such questions as: 'can I park nearby?' or 'if I go to that store, can I get everything I need (= saving time)?' or 'that store offers the best choice at the right price', and so on. In the case of online stores, questions to do with delivery times and returning goods will arise. Even when shopping just for fun, people still imagine in advance which shops they definitely want to go to: because of familiarity or force of habit, to boost their self-esteem, for hedonistic reasons or whatever.

In other words, the mental shortlist people make will to a large extent determine the shops they ultimately go to. The very fact that you can choose a store from the comfort of your own home is because of the store's identity, its personality and brand value. The initial choice is based on the senses: sights, sounds, smells, tastes and feel. These are used as a basis for making personal choices. This is why the way in which stores manifest themselves, in terms of the various senses, is so important. It enables us to remember the stores and to recall the experiences we felt.
One store that has a strong appeal to the senses is Lush. You can imagine the handwritten signs, the colours and containers in your mind's eye, as well as the soaps displayed like enormous cheeses and all the scents and fragrances that always penetrate the stores and even reach out into the street.

This sensual experience is one area of added value where the physical store beats its online counterpart: however useful online shopping may be, it is still impossible to achieve the complete, sensual shopping experience in the virtual world. There are also other aspects of a physical store that are still difficult to read or interpret online: the spirit and atmosphere of the store, the people who frequent it, for example, but you can also identify the type of store from its scale and format as well as the specializations of the retailer, all of which are obvious at a glance. On the internet, almost every retailer is identical: whether you can find it is largely determined by online search engines and its format exists within the grid of the website.

The mental shortlist people make will to a large extent determine the shops they ultimately go to.

It should now be obvious that a retail brand needs to find a place on the consumer's shortlist in order to become known by the consumer and his peers. But that is not an easy process. Besides, getting the consumer's attention is made more difficult by the fact that there is so much on offer within physical or virtual reach of the consumer. The customer journey is all about being known. If the consumers don't know your store, they will probably never visit it. And if they never visit it, they will definitely not buy anything at it. Knowing and appreciating will ensure that the essential relationship develops between the consumer and the retailer and this in turn will guide the consumer to the store and towards the ultimate purchase or transaction.

Let's take the example of a man who wants to buy a suit. He sets off, having already decided on the first shop he wants to visit. It's a major store, offering a wide choice and with both a men's and women's department. Once in the high street, he can see the store from a distance. This impression must ultimately be an extension of the feeling he had about the store while still at home. Physically, visually and even at a distance, the store will need to live up to that impression and preferably surpass it. He is then standing outside the store. The window displays, the product presentations and the initial communication create an immediate experience of the store brand. On entering, the actual embracing takes place. The total atmosphere of the retail brand now takes control and the thought that was conceived at home on the sofa becomes a reality. He recalls what he has come for and the distinction between the men's and women's departments makes it clear where he needs to be: the same identity, but a different atmosphere. In the men's department, he recognizes the brand identity of the casuals department on the one hand and the business wear department on the other. The latter is much more formal than the jeans and T-shirts in the casual section. He walks towards the department selling suits. Gradually, the product becomes more important than the retailer as the customer zooms in. He sees the retailer's own label and a number of brands, perhaps Armani, Boss and Breuer. With designer brands, the atmosphere of the brand becomes more important than that of the shop and Armani or Boss can add their own distinctive cachet to the store brand. But they must be in the right place, with a product that is relevant. If this man needs it, virtual social shopping can also play an active role during the purchasing process. As people spend more and more time on the mobile internet and become increasingly

181

active in doing so, initiatives such as Tweet Mirror and Go Try It On have emerged. Whilst trying on the suits, he can take a photo of himself in a potential new outfit. If he instantly sends the photograph via Twitter, people can respond to the outfit and have an immediate influence on his decision whether or not to purchase it.

When he has chosen the suit, he steps back into the atmosphere of the store and perhaps chooses another product, after repeating the stages of the Retail Choice Diagram©.

The example describes all the steps the consumer takes, which apply whether he is buying a suit or a toothbrush: the consumer needs to be enticed or seduced into the store. Moreover, these steps also apply online, because the same phases and choices leading up to a purchase also need to happen on the website. Between each step in the process, it is up to the retailer to maintain or strengthen the link with the consumer or to break it, leaving the consumer to his own fate.

THE RETAIL CHOICE DIAGRAM© FROM THE RETAILER'S PERSPECTIVE

THE RETAIL CHOICE DIAGRAM© PROVIDES GUIDANCE TO THE RETAILER IN APPROACHING CONSUMERS.

At every step, the retailer must create points of contact and preferably help the consumer in the choices that face him or her. Completing all the levels of the Retail Choice Diagram© involves both a rational and an emotional approach. From an emotional perspective, all the communications will of course need to project the identity of the retail brand and draw the customer almost unconsciously into the store. These signals will then lead the customer to the right department and ultimately to the product he came for. This guiding power comes from the different layers created by applying the steps of the Retail Choice Diagram©; there are continuous shifts of focus as the message continually targets the consumer's mindset. In this way, the customer is literally guided on his journey through the store. Only if all levels have been completed will the customer journey flow properly. From a rational perspective, it is more like a retailer's checklist. Have all the steps been completed? And is the relationship being properly pursued? Within this relationship, the retailer first asks for attention, gains it when the consumer comes to the store for this attention and in the store the retailer will need to give the customer the personal attention he demands.

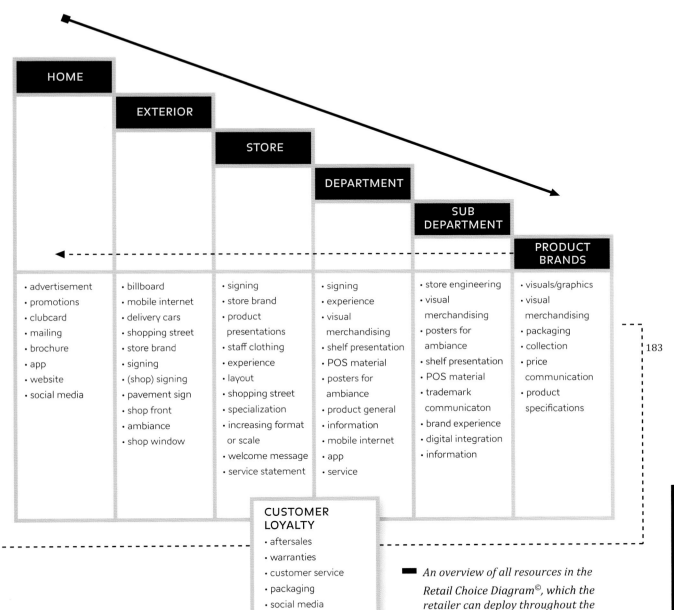

HOME	EXTERIOR	STORE	DEPARTMENT	SUB DEPARTMENT	PRODUCT BRANDS
• advertisement • promotions • clubcard • mailing • brochure • app • website • social media	• billboard • mobile internet • delivery cars • shopping street • store brand • signing • (shop) signing • pavement sign • shop front • ambiance • shop window	• signing • store brand • product presentations • staff clothing • experience • layout • shopping street • specialization • increasing format or scale • welcome message • service statement	• signing • experience • visual merchandising • shelf presentation • POS material • posters for ambiance • product general • information • mobile internet • app • service	• store engineering • visual merchandising • posters for ambiance • shelf presentation • POS material • trademark communicaton • brand experience • digital integration • information	• visuals/graphics • visual merchandising • packaging • collection • price communication • product specifications

CUSTOMER LOYALTY
- aftersales
- warranties
- customer service
- packaging
- social media
- clubcard
- direct mail
- loyalty programs

An overview of all resources in the Retail Choice Diagram©, which the retailer can deploy throughout the customer journey.

Ask for attention, gain attention, give attention; the retailer must first capture the attention of the consumer. When the consumer comes to the store, the retailer will need to give the customer the personal attention he or she demands.

Asking for attention is about publicity and advertising methods, a mass-media approach to promotion. On the one hand, these methods are rational in their intention: weekly offers or the announcement of a new product launch ultimately aim to attract people to the store. But they are also emotional in nature: the retailer is attempting to convey its brand personality. The mass-media communications that consumers encounter at home and out and about (leaflets, brochures, billboards, advertisements in magazines and newspapers, on TV and the internet, apps, etc.) must be related to what happens in the store.

Gaining attention is all about the customers' response: their decision to come to the store. The expectations and imaginary image created must be something that consumers can recognize in the street scene (advertising, signs, etc.) and through the personality radiating from the store (logo, frontage, window displays, etc.). Out-of-store communication will more closely reflect the iconography and identity of the retailer. It is all about the architecture of the building, the signing leading to it and possibly a large banner as you drive towards it. For stores on the outskirts of the city in particular, these three elements play an important role. The freedom in terms of architecture that has developed in such areas enables retailers to express their personality through highly characteristic and recognizable buildings. For some retailers, this is precisely the reason why they choose locations outside the city. The iconography they use tends to be very direct since the cars flashing past need to be able to recognize or identify the retailer in just a few seconds. Of course, some of the best-known examples are IKEA's blue box and the yellow M of McDonalds. Out-of-store communication also involves such things as: delivery vehicles, the external sign (dynamic sign), the entrance sign, window displays (with visual merchandising) and posters, all of this possibly complete with publicity announcements (with a tone that reflects the brand personality, of course).

Top left: on the street, a retail brand attracts the attention of consumers. The motorway is a great location, because people are usually bored in their cars. BCC trucks have a strong visual impact (right).

Top right: the architecture of buildings guides consumers on the customer journey, so they know they are at the right place. McDonalds does this by integrating its brand icon into the building (top left).

Below: Once at the retailer, it is important that the customer gains the retailer's attention (below). The customer will then leave the shop with a positive feeling and is more likely to return.

185

9. THE CUSTOMER JOURNEY

Giving attention places the initiative back in the hands of the retailer. The customer has arrived and says: 'You called me. Here I am, so show me something.' This is the moment of truth. The store itself will need to convey its message by means of its functional layout and functional communication. In-store communication is very important in supporting the process of choice. Clear information that distinguishes between different brands and products ensures that the customer knows which product is best suited for the intended purpose. In addition, communication relating to the brand personality is also advantageous. Many stores have a tendency to repeat the publicity advertising again in the store, with the same mass-media tone, even though a more individual tone is what is now needed. Ultimately, in-store communication replaces the long-lost shopkeeper, who knew exactly what his specific customer wanted and provided information, personalized offers and ingenious presentations. What is needed here is a translation of the mass-media language into a more personal style of communication. The message must be made relevant to the individual in order to convince him or her to proceed towards the transaction.

THE PURCHASE IS NOT THE END OF THE JOURNEY

Giving attention is not only about the process of buying. For retailers, the after-sales stage of the customer journey is becoming increasingly important because this is the phase in which customers share their experiences and opinions with others. Experiences that occur later in the buying process have significant impact in terms of creating the customer's opinions and memories, if only because this final impression may overshadow previous experiences. After-sales includes practical issues such as the home delivery of an online

order, in-store collection, exchanges, service and guarantees. Starting to use the product after purchase is another important moment. It presents the retailer with another opportunity to surprise the customer. The moment of unpacking is so important precisely because it often involves a feeling of enthusiasm. As a retailer, it is in your interest to emphasize this feeling at that moment. If the product has been bought online, unpacking can be even more important, because it is the first physical introduction to the brand. At this moment, the customer has a specific expectation of the product, based on the images seen online: this needs to be fulfilled or surpassed. In this case, there is an interval between the times when the customer buys, receives and first uses the product, a major difference from physical retail. This lack of instant fulfilment creates a gap in the customer journey. The chain is temporarily broken, which means that when the purchase is delivered at the home, the customer's mindset could have changed completely since buying the product (as an impulse or planned purchase). This is very likely to influence how the product is judged, possibly leading to its being returned. You should also never underestimate the importance of the delivery person. To a certain extent this person determines the first impression in this stage of the customer journey. In the physical store, serious attention is paid to recruiting and training suitable staff, who have the right image and embrace the brand philosophy. However, in online retail, delivery is often completely outsourced. The retailer loses control over brand surveillance and intended quality. In such cases, delivery is no longer part of the brand or the platform development, even though it should be. In the after-sales stage, there are certainly possibilities for the retailer to trigger the customer's enthusiasm again, to recapture what was felt at the time of purchase. Or perhaps even better, to maintain the customer's enthusiasm during the period of waiting.

But after-sales service is also extremely important. Any complaints or comments from the customer must be taken seriously and suitable solutions must be found. The very fact that the customer can share any negative experiences with the masses makes it essential that he is kept happy in this stage. Mutual trust is very important in this. It may seem obvious that it is important for the customer to trust the retailer, but the retailer also needs to trust the customer not to abuse the position of power he has acquired. This is also the case in practice: the customer understands the importance of reciprocity. In any case, unjustified, negative comments about products and services are often refuted by enthusiastic users. By engaging in dialogue with the customer, criticism and comments can be used as valuable input for modifications and product optimization. This also gives the consumer a feeling of being taken seriously and valued. If this valuable contact is sustained, he will be more likely to remain loyal to the retail brand.

This delivery service knows its business!

OMNI-CHANNEL STRATEGY

In today's retail 3.0, the consumer has the upper hand and it is increasingly difficult for the retailer to gain his attention and keep it. The relationship with consumers needs to be configured in a unique and distinctive way. To gain attention, the retailer will need to have presence in more different places. The retailer needs to surprise the consumer on his journey: at home, out and about and on the internet. In order to gain attention, the retailer needs to do even better than best since consumers have high expectations in terms of the attention they receive from the retailer. Instead of one-way traffic, the consumer wants interaction, and to enter into dialogue with the retailer.

On any day, the consumer faces a flood of information and is only able to process a limited amount of it. This means making choices, so he looks for confirmation and direction in making the right choices. The retailer needs to provide the customer with support during the customer journey and to help him or her to make the right choices. By offering relevant information at the right times and via the right sources, the retailer can ensure that the customer's process of choice is clearer and easier, giving him or her a feeling of doing the right thing. The more effectively the brand can provide coaching in this, the more it will be valued.

In order to work in this kind of interactive way, retail organizations require completely different operations. Operations that are flexible and demand-driven and focused on the customer. However, existing processes and distribution within organizations are often driven by supply and procurement and are not equipped to achieve the changes needed in retail.

Whatever happens, the retailer must ensure that its different activities and points of contact are linked together in a holistic way throughout the enormously varied customer journey. Rather than seeing each individual channel as a separate medium with its own related strategy, all of the channels must combine to create the total brand experience. With the idea of the brand as the central proposition, the activities in offline and online retail must repeatedly link together and reinforce each other in an integrated way.

> *The omni-channel strategy enables the retailer to get closer to the consumer, in a way that is relevant to him or her.*

This process and the matching strategy may vary for each type of product. It will depend on the frequency of purchase, the emotion involved in the product and the purchase and the alternatives available. This integrated approach gives the consumer the opportunity to obtain information via several channels simultaneously and to purchase a product or service in numerous completely different places and ways.

This so-called omni-channel strategy enables the retailer to get closer to the consumer. The possibilities offered by the internet and digitalization provide the customer with the alternative to find information about the brand and assortment and to purchase it online. But by using social media

Le Pain Quotidien has pop-up bars on the street alongside the cafes, seen here in New York City.

and especially mobile shopping media, the retailer can also play an increasing role in supporting customer choice. These media can be used at any random point and in every phase of the customer journey in order to win over the consumer by offering sufficient added value wherever they are and in whatever mood they may be.

The omni-channel philosophy also involves operating several different store formats and sales channels. In order to be where the customer is and anticipate his mood, mindset and needs at that time, it increasingly seems that retail formulas need to become dynamic. Retail is becoming increasingly difficult within a uniform or single format, since the store and the proposition run the risk of becoming too generic: it is not possible to be relevant and provide the desired attention for every need and for everyone all of the time. This is why increasing numbers of retailers are developing different store formats and points of contact with consumers, with an offer and proposition that is fine-tuned to suit the specific location and people who frequent it. All of these different types of store combine to form the retail formula. Alongside a regular store type, there may for example be a small local store, a city concept, a 'to go' concept and a webshop.

One example of this is the British supermarket chain Tesco. By operating several different formats and channels, Tesco is able to cater for a wide variety of consumer needs. What's more, the group also claims that this gives it the flexibility it needs to respond to local markets.

The retail formula should be seen as the totality of a company's activities. What characterizes these activities is the focus on an one-to-one relationship between the brand and the consumer. The possibilities for this go far further than the store alone. The more points of contact there are with the consumer, the more intensive the relationship becomes, as the consumer is reminded more frequently of the brand and the brand in turn can play an added value role more often. This then increases customer loyalty.

For the customer too, this variety of points of contact and formats becomes much more surprising and inspirational than just a single type of store that, especially in the case of a chain store, is more or less the same everywhere. The very uniformity of retail chains is what makes almost

Digitization is bringing an increase in all kinds of customized retailing. At the Tate Modern Museum (top left), you can order art and have it delivered at home. In the Nike ID Studio (bottom left), you can design your own sneakers. Convenience concepts are emerging alongside regular store formats, such as Muji to Go (top right) and Marks & Spencer Simply Food (bottom right).

For consumers, the variety of contact points is surprising and inspirational.

every city high street look the same. On the one hand, this can be useful for us as consumers because brand recognition means we know exactly what to expect in the store and whether or not it is where we want to be. If you're looking for some new jeans, you know in advance which stores to go to. But on the other hand, it can make shopping monotonous and efficient rather than presenting us with a challenge to try out something different. This uniform presence of the retailer makes the relationship between the brand and the consumer into one-way traffic, where the offer is simply pushed by the retailer. The consumer has to adapt to what the high street has to offer. If the consumer doesn't want to, he must find a better alternative. In retail 3.0, this power relationship will need to change.

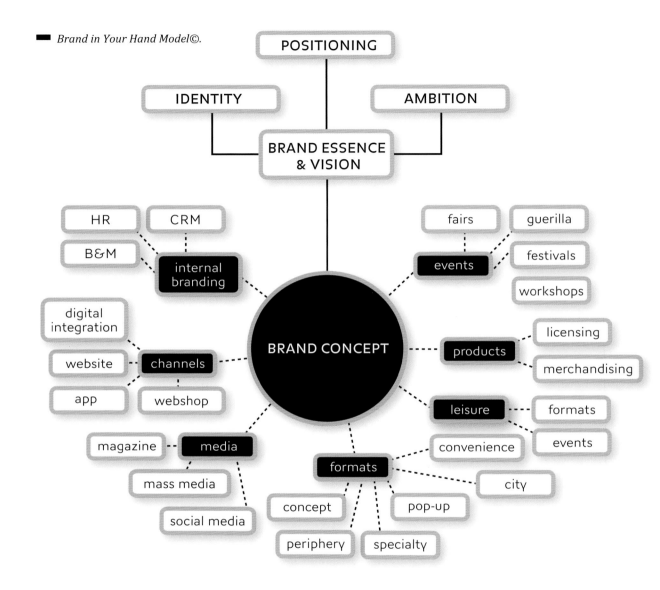

Brand in Your Hand Model©.

BRAND PERSONALITY AS THE STARTING POINT

For a retailer to be able to adapt to consumer behaviour and play a meaningful role in as many situations as possible, transparency is an important precondition for survival. Moreover, the retailer needs to be where the consumer is and provide access to the information he needs.

Throughout the customer journey, the brand must have a consistent and coherent impact. As the retailer makes its omni-channel strategy part of the consumer's world, creating multiple, relevant customer contact points, the customer will see it as a strong brand and brand personality. In an effective omni-channel strategy, the different market activities flow into each other, creating a consistent brand experience.

With that in mind, it is important to develop a versatile formula: if you apply brand personality reasoning, it becomes possible to imagine what this personality could do and what would suit it. This personality then becomes a source of inspiration. Of course, all the activities must match the brand and emerge from the brand definition. The closer the connection to the consumer, the more versatile and multifaceted the brand can be. This is because the consumer's commitment and interest will draw his attention to the various retail activities, which he will then understand and appreciate. The Brand In Your Hand Model© provides guidance in this. It includes a variety of online and offline, physical and virtual elements, which can be loaded with the brand. These work together in an integrated way to form the brand image for the consumer. The model presents increased opportunities to explore the brand's potential for the target group. In many cases, this

potential extends beyond the core business, creating space for thought, continuity and a vision for the future. An added advantage is that this way of thinking gives the organization and all its staff an enormous drive, because working for the future is inspiring and fulfilling.

After exploring the options, the Platform Model© can be used to configure the omni-channel strategy. Based on the development of the store concept, the brand and its ambition gradually become clear and take shape. Even the outermost rings of the model, which represent the external forces, have already been identified. With this knowledge and input, it is possible to brainstorm on how each section, each retail element should be configured by examining what fits the brand and what doesn't. This is not so much about agreeing the details for regular stores, but more specifically for other channels too. The holistic effect of the model also ensures that a brand has a balanced presence in the market and is represented in all areas.

In this case, brand management is essential. Make sure you know what you are doing and ensure that the recipient also understands it. In order to achieve this, the brand image and brand identity need to be the same, as the Brand In Your Hand Model© shows. The brand needs to be consistent in the way it is communicated at any particular time, but also in the longer term. As we said earlier: It is no easy task becoming number one, and even more difficult staying there.

SHOPPING BEHAVIOUR

"Retail is fundamentally critical because no matter how hard you work at developing great products there is little point if you cannot connect them with your shopper."

LARS THOMASSEN IN 'RETAILIZATION'

194

DESPITE KNOWING THE DESIRES, CONSIDERATIONS AND LIFESTYLES OF CONSUMERS, AND DESPITE THOROUGH TARGET GROUP RESEARCH, CONSUMER BEHAVIOUR REMAINS LARGELY UNPREDICTABLE.

By no means does every shopper (visitor to the store) become a customer (purchaser). There is much debate about shopper insight, about how people shop, what they do and do not experience, how their moods affect them and so on, but the factors that influence shopping behaviour all come down to five basic human characteristics. These five characteristics express themselves to a greater or lesser degree in different situations and at different times, and they dominate in different ways in different people.

Firstly, people are only capable of processing a limited amount of information at a time. It is said that at most, we remember a maximum of seven things in a series at once, while in reality, a continuous flood of new information is of course always reaching us at any given time. We do not register most of that information at all, and we have different ways of clustering information and giving it meaning. Our memories are trained to automate these processes, so that they consume less effort and less of our capacity to process them. Recognizing something is therefore important in clustering information, because associations can be made with earlier experiences. Concentration also plays an important role. When we have a certain objective in mind, we are far less open to other stimuli. We scan through a store, as it were, in search of the items on our shopping list. Examples commonly referred to as illustrations of our focus and concentration include a film in which a basketball team is filmed from above. The players were asked to count how often the ball was passed from player to player. They easily came up with the correct answer, but when they were asked if they had seen the man in a monkey suit running amongst the players, they all replied that they had not seen him at all.

In his book, Why We Buy, Paco Underhill illustrates this principle with a retail situation. Chocolate bars are dispersed at different locations in a supermarket, as 'impulse products'. One of these locations is in the pet foods section. It soon becomes obvious that this does not work as a location for selling chocolate, simply because there is no clear connection between pet foods and chocolate. Here, people are focused on what they need for their dog or cat. Those who do not have a pet will pay no attention at all to this section and, because they are not focused on it, they will not even see the chocolate bars.

A second characteristic is that we find it difficult to make choices. Every day, we are overloaded with all kinds of brand and product information, much of which is indistinguishable from the rest. This means that making choices is increasingly more difficult and, in principle, more time-consuming. We consider it extremely important to feel that we are making the right choice. This is because of our third human characteristic, which is our need for a personal overview and personal

control. We need this in order to have a sense of security. Human beings therefore have a tendency to make rapid associations and to categorize. This is primarily based on experience, but knowledge and acquired information can be strong factors in influencing this process. Because we want to avoid risks, we are happy to respond to the recommendations and experiences of others. If many other people, even though they are strangers, are enthusiastic about a certain product, brand or store, then it will be a safe bet to go along with them. Going along with other people's experiences also helps us make choices more rapidly.

Indeed, as all this is going on, today's information inundation continues to flood over us, via more and more different channels. Verbal information is being increasingly replaced by images and symbols. Visually, more information can be conveyed. In our discussion of design, in Chapter 1, we spoke about how visual images have become increasingly important. For retail, the consequence of this is that consumers want to be well informed, in a ready-to-digest form, one that is reliable and authentic. Here, visual identity and consistency are of major significance, because they create our points of recognition, including brand associations.

Fourthly, people expect empathy and acknowledgement. They want to be supported in the process of making their choices, so that making a selection is as easy as possible. This needs to happen in such a way that they feel in complete control of the selection process, which is why authenticity and a clear brand personality are so important. People want to see that there is an understanding of their needs and desires, that they are being taken seriously. They do not want to feel that they are being made fun of or taken advantage of, but that they have in fact made the right choice. On the other hand, consumers are easily bored or distracted, and they need new stimuli to inspire them. In short, consumers are forever curious. Because of all the information they have to process every single day, it is more and more difficult to keep their attention. For this reason, it is very important that the information we give them is consistent. If information is inconsistent or not in line with the brand, the associations with that brand and with other information will not immediately be made, and consumers' attention will tend to wander. Additionally, information that is already familiar to them will just be ignored as their crucial focus shifts to new stimuli.

The Dutch retail expert, Henk Gianotten, has developed this theory of 'the comfort of the known and the excitement of the new'. His concept is that people are always looking for a certain balance between the known and the unknown. 'The known' ensures ease and a sense of control and security, while 'the unknown' brings excitement and sensation. Too much of the known generates boredom, while too much of the unknown incites stress and feelings of insecurity. One has to strike a balance between these two extremes, and this balance depends on both personality traits and situational characteristics. Older people more often seek the comfort of what is familiar to them, while adventurous people are more enthusiastic about unknown situations. When we are in a hurry, we appreciate a familiar situation, and when we are actually out to enjoy shopping, we want to be stimulated by new and unusual experiences. In other words, in developing a store formula, it is important to accurately chart the target group, in order to find the right balance between the comfort of the known and the excitement of the new.

▬ *A friendly message from Uniqlo: we provide an appropriate range, you only need to bring your body.*

"Consumers are looking for the comfort of the known and the excitement of the new."

HENK GIANOTTEN, DIRECTOR OF PANTEIA

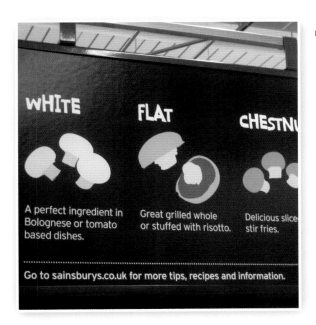

Left: the vegetable department at Sainsbury's supermarket explains the difference between the various mushrooms to help the customer choose.

Below: Sephora gives a clear overview of the total range of makeup accessories.

10.
RETAIL COMPLEXITY

Constantly changing dynamics

ABOUT THE LOVE FOR RETAIL, ENTREPRENEURSHIP, THE DESIRE TO MOVE WITH THE TIMES, THE EMOTIONAL BOND WITH THE CUSTOMER, AN EQUAL AND INTERACTIVE ONE-TO-ONE RELATIONSHIP, CREATIVITY AND INNOVATION AS DISTINCTIVE WEAPONS, ABOUT THE GLOBAL WORLD AND THE LOCAL MARKET, ABOUT BRAND ACTIVATION THROUGHOUT THE FORMULA, THE EVERLASTING ESSENCE OF RETAIL, THE NEED FOR CONSISTENCY AND COHERENCE AND ABOUT THE FORMULA FOR SUCCESS IN SHOPPING AREAS.

WHILE THE CLOCK IS TICKING

the world changes.

Love transcends the complexity of retail. Art, seen in New York City.

WHAT MAKES RETAIL SO CHALLENGING IS THAT IT IS CONTINUALLY CHANGING AND NO TWO DAYS ARE THE SAME.

Retail is unbelievably complicated because it depends on so many factors: external influences beyond the control of the retailer that continually change the behaviour of potential buyers and the fact that the market and competition are always on the move. In order to remain relevant and distinctive both in the market and for the consumer, the retailer needs to continually anticipate the changing world. In order to do this, he needs to develop, implement and maintain the internal factors, all of the retail elements, at the same time and cohesively. The Platform Development Model©, the theme running throughout this book, provides insight into the cohesion, dynamism and complexity of retail and visualizes the one-to-one relationship between the retailer and his context.

Change is essential in the fight for survival and as a means of maintaining and even intensifying this relationship. Passion for the business is what drives the retailer and motivates him or her to build a valuable personal relationship with the customers, to find out what will create customer loyalty and entice the customer to the store again and again. This passion rubs off on customers. But it is not solely limited to the store: the customer journey© is a highly important part of the relationship and the success of the retailer.
By properly responding to the different mindsets of the consumer during the purchasing process, the retailer can accompany the consumer to the virtual and/or physical store. For this, the retailer

needs to be present at every step in the customer journey, creating a consistent and coherent series of brand activities. The retailer's passion for his business acts as the seducer, and is unique and distinct from that of other players.

This passion for the business is an internal value that transcends everything since a passionate retailer will be recognized and appreciated by consumers. Some retailers focus perhaps too much on turnover and earning money and base their reasoning on the possibilities of logistics and organization. They run the risk of becoming conservative and continuing along the same path for as long as things go well and sufficient money is being earned. This wait-and-see attitude makes you little more than a follower in the market and you are unlikely to stand out from the crowd. At worst, your position in the market will become weaker and when you realize it, it may be too late to turn things around. This is why it is important to remain on the move, to continue to innovate, move with the times, develop and try out new things.

Retailers whose main focus is business as usual tend to be the traditional type, driven by purchasing: they buy things at a good price, based on previous success within the company and then sell it at a good margin. Offering a lower price is what distinguishes them from the competition. We believe that this is a dead-end route, which pushes price margins to their limit, but offers nothing in the way of added value or genuine distinction.

And what does the consumer do in response? He becomes increasingly less loyal, always looking for the lowest price, because there is little emotional connection and everything is about price.

"You must attack at all times. Listen to Johan Cruijff: 'If you want to stay ahead, you put another attacker on the pitch.' As a boss and the company, you must attack, always attack. You must continually innovate. Take the lead in everything, from positioning to pricing. You need to be the first in digital communication."

KEVIN ROBERTS, CEO WORLDWIDE OF SAATCHI & SAATCHI

This makes shopping less personal because the relationship becomes monotonous and loses its intensity.

Action, a fast-growing low-cost store in the Netherlands has however shown that the combination of lowest price and putting the consumer first is actually possible: whereas many retailers base their sales price on the purchase price plus a good margin, Action bases its prices on what it expects the customer will want to pay. In order to do that, the company needs to have a good understanding of what the customer wants.

Action therefore does targeted purchasing from wholesalers rather than picking up cheap consignments from the Far East. Thanks to its sophisticated purchasing and pricing strategy, Action manages to be around 35% cheaper than the competition. There are good reasons why Action is a feared player in the market. What makes it really smart is that it has a highly-varied and rapidly changing offer, which enables it to take on the competition across a wide market. But it always targets a different part of that wide market,

making the company unpredictable and difficult to copy. It is also hard for the competition to respond to Action: if you decide to counter with a competing promotion because Action has stolen all your customers one week, you may find it's too late, because Action will already be competing with new products in a different segment. Thanks to the wide-ranging, fast-changing assortment, with 100 to 150 new products in the store each week, the consumer is also guaranteed to be surprised every week. This in turn ensures that they go there.

In today's retail 3.0 age, the customer has the upper hand: push has become pull or even interaction. The consumer decides where, what and when to buy. The internet and comparison websites have massively increased price transparency. They also offer extensive information about the potential purchase, originating from the brand, from retailers and through other consumers' reviews. The consumer is therefore better informed about what is available and what he wants. He is aware of the choices available and this wide-ranging offering makes it more difficult for retailers to stand out from the crowd and make sure that the consumer chooses them.

Because everything is available 24/7 on the internet, retailers need to become driven by demand rather than supply. The days of take it or leave it in retail are long gone. The stores (whatever form they take) need to offer what the customer is looking for: it's not about selling the things you have, but the customer buying what he wants. The assortment and the service need to reflect the needs of consumers. This is how to attract them to your store. Above all, the retailer needs to surprise them, and know how to provide them with added value.

■ *Interaction creates equality between the retailer and consumer. Eataly includes this in its policy.*

> ## *"Innovation is the holy grail in retail. As the tart doesn't become bigger, every retailer wants to put the competition out of business."*
>
> **RODNEY FITCH**

It is only possible to surprise someone if you know them and know how to surprise them. Surprising people needs to be something clever and well thought-through, not a longshot in the hope that you may make someone happy.
By being creative, you can shape your one-to-one relationship with the customer.

For many retailers, the shift from supply to demand is a major step. By doing this, retailers are responding to consumers, but an one-to-one relationship involves more: one-to-one is actually about equality and two-way traffic. In the new world of retail, the customer has a real role. Starbucks understands how to achieve this. This café chain has grown to become popular worldwide. As a way of thanking the customers for their contribution to this, Starbucks has launched various different initiatives to do something in return for people and the world. One of these is the 'Create Jobs for USA' programme, to reduce American unemployment by protecting jobs and generating new ones. As part of this, the company has promised to open more branches in America and to update many of its existing cafes.

By launching these projects, Starbucks can employ more people. In addition, Starbucks is making substantial funding available for capital grants for ailing local companies, in the form of salaries, micro-credits and the funding of community centres and house-building.

But Starbucks is also asking something of consumers. 'My Starbucks Idea' is a way of asking people to explain about their lives, how they see the future of Starbucks and what they would like

A leaflet explains how Starbucks will generate jobs in the United States.

204

to see changed. Since Starbucks then actually showcases the ideas that have been realized, people become involved and eager to take part themselves. Of course, this also serves as a highly valuable source of inspiration for Starbucks.

A vision for the future, innovation and creativity are essential. They enable added value to be created. As Seth Godin's book 'Linchpin: Are you indispensable?' suggests, many aspects of an organization can be replicated or copied. Products

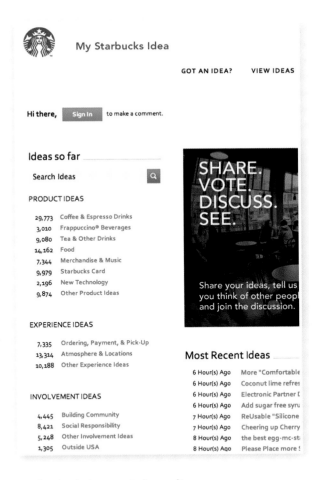

■ Starbucks has created an online platform where people can share ideas for the brand.

> # *"It is creativity that makes a company indispensable, unforgettable and impossible to replicate."*
>
> **SETH GODIN IN 'LINCHPIN'**

can be manufactured more cheaply in China. It is more financially advantageous to base your factories in low-wage countries. You can even outsource certain services to cheaper players in the market. But it is creativity that makes the company indispensable, unforgettable and impossible to replicate. The same applies to retailers: you can buy anything cheaper or more quickly on the internet. But a unique experience, a special version of the one-to-one relationship between brand and consumer, in which creativity is used to achieve an effect, means that people will take the time and effort needed to come to you. This is an important cornerstone in a retailer's right to exist.

Consumers want to be able to identify with the product, the store and the people in the company. The store identity therefore needs to closely reflect their interests and the lifestyle they aspire to. This is why the consumer wants to see the human side of the brand. It appeals to him or her and what he stands for. This again emphasizes that companies should not only focus on the lowest price: that is a rational value, but the customer is actually looking for emotion. The Retail Formula© shows that the retail brand is made up of a combination of rational and emotional values. The rational values are the unique selling points, supplemented by the authentic brand values or emotional selling points that cannot be copied. The retailers that continually innovate, surprise and invest in the relationship are the winners: these are the retailers for whom customers are willing to stand in line. This calls for real entrepreneurship. It is dynamic, as dynamic as the changing world and changing consumer behaviour. And because, in retail, the effects of what you do are always immediately noticeable in the conversion, entrepreneurship is the ideal approach: try it out in one or two stores, check out the effects and make adjustments if it doesn't work as well as hoped. In order to be a contemporary retailer, reticence and a conservative approach need to make way for innovation. Innovation in 360° retail, in all the aspects reflected in the Platform Development Model©.

"There is hardly anything in the world that some man cannot make a little worse and sell a little cheaper."

JOHN RUSKIN (1819-1900)

206

■ *The Retail Formula©.*

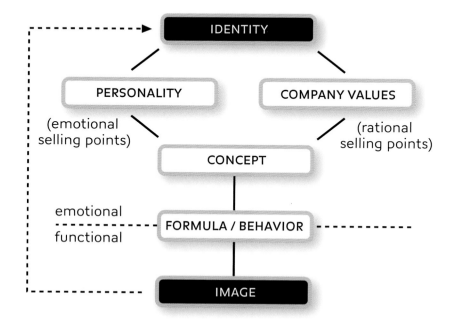

360° RETAILING

NESPRESSO IS A GOOD EXAMPLE OF A 360° RETAILER THAT EFFECTIVELY IMPLEMENTS AND CONTROLS EVERY ASPECT OF ITS RETAIL BUSINESS.

Nespresso has redefined the way in which coffee drinkers enjoy their espresso coffee. It is a quick and easy way of making delicious coffee. Thanks to a closed system of espresso machine and coffee capsules, it is possible to equal the quality of the barista every time. By doing this, Nespresso is offering quality, convenience and volume tailored to the customer. It is a major breakthrough in the coffee culture which previously involved making a large jug of filter coffee or, in the case of Nescafe, the mother of Nespresso, simply instant coffee.

The company's passion is to create quality and continue to strive to innovate. This is not only focused on the product, the capsules and machines, but on all aspects of the company. Nespresso wants to bring pleasure to people who love coffee and this is a clear indication that they are putting the customer first. Customer service is an important cornerstone of the brand.

Nespresso was originally targeted at the business market and its products can be ordered through the Nespresso Club. When Nespresso also entered the consumer market, physical sales outlets were opened: the Nespresso Boutiques and Boutique-in-shops. The store concept offers a strong and exclusive brand experience. In the run-up to the opening, there is always wrapping around the building and the capsules play a key role (see illustration XX). Even after the opening of the Boutique, the capsules feature prominently in the store: the panels behind the counters are completely covered with coloured capsules, representing the different coffee blends. On the shop floor, there is a major focus on the range of machines and accessories and a coffee bar with seating where people can try out the coffee. The staff are professional and highly service-oriented. They are supported by the Nespresso Club customer profiles, in which all previous purchases are recorded. This enables the staff to remind you each time of the flavour you like most and to base their recommendations on this. The same happens if you order online or via the app. You then have a choice of collecting your purchase in a Boutique (after just one hour), at a special collection point or to have it delivered by a Nespresso courier. The online Nespresso Club gives you access to the customer service and repair service.

207

Nespresso in New York City.

10. THE COMPLEXITY OF RETAIL

Nespresso has also set itself a number of targets concerning sustainability and environmental pollution. It has developed its own recycling system in order to make a contribution to processing the waste created by the coffee capsules. Once used, the capsules can be handed in at the Boutiques, at the collection points or given to the courier. But the company has also launched a number of projects to preserve the planet's resources for future generations.

The brand has earned itself a strong position. Because the product is not available in just any store, it offers an exclusive experience, which has created a certain cachet. People have an active attitude towards the brand and are willing to stand in line in the stores. By fully controlling all aspects of the formula, Nespresso ensures that the concept is effectively executed and any modifications can be rapidly implemented. The store image and brand experience is the same across the world.

Good innovation is applied 360°, and is recognizable anywhere.

Nespresso as a 360° retailer plotted in the ■ *Platform Development Model©.*

GLOBAL VERSUS LOCAL

THE WHOLE WORLD IS WITHIN REACH. BECAUSE WE NEARLY ALWAYS HAVE ACCESS TO THE INTERNET ALMOST ANYWHERE, WE CAN FIND OUT ABOUT THE LATEST NEWS IN AN INSTANT, CONTACT FRIENDS, AND LET OTHERS KNOW WHAT WE LIKE AND WHAT WE'RE DOING.

Information spreads rapidly and the internet means that our surroundings are actually the whole world. Changes also seem to happen faster because we hear about things that we would not otherwise have heard. These changes also influence consumers, making their behaviour and needs change faster and more frequently.

As well as information, we also become aware of what is available everywhere in the world. This global supply means that it is possible to develop one's own direction and tastes within the whole. Customers can form their own opinions. If they can't find what they're looking for, they carry on looking, because they know that there is more. Increasing numbers of brands are offering customization options in order to better anticipate the individual tastes and wishes of the customer.

On the downside, this enormous supply and connection with the whole world can be overwhelming. Just as trends can trigger counter-movements, the response to globalization is also an increasing demand for things on a smaller scale and local involvement. There are a number of reasons for this.

There is increasing awareness of the negative impact on the environment of international trade, travel and mass production, for example.

In response, there are more and more initiatives involving the exclusive use of organic and environmentally-friendly products and local suppliers as a way of reducing the CO_2 emissions caused by distribution. A nice example of this is the French company Kbane. This DIY store helps people to make their homes healthier, more energy-efficient and environmentally-friendlier. It has eco-coaches who provide personal advice and who will then make the modifications in your home, or you can do it yourself. The products are sustainable and environmentally-friendly and Kbane aims to ensure that its stores are as sustainable as possible by using solar panels, wind turbines and collecting rainwater.

Globalization and the individualization of society have developed alongside each other as people have become less dependent on their immediate environment and more able to shape their own needs. The focus has shifted to self-actualization, the fourth layer of the Maslov pyramid. The possibility of being independent in society and pursuing one's own course is an extremely valuable right, but the need for commitment to one's immediate environment is also increasing: the feeling of belonging and the feeling of having a pleasant home environment. The popularity of local communities, initiatives and specialist stores is increasing. Involvement in the local community and the personal aspect is appealing because of its contrast to the big, impersonal world.

In retail too, increasing numbers of stores are part of a national or international chain. Wherever they may be, these chains usually all look the same. This more or less rules out any real local involvement. Often the store is remote,

even though the consumer has a need for a personal approach and personal assistance from someone who knows them from previous visits. The consumer is looking for a special assortment that suits his own wishes. McDonalds is developing heavily in this area. First of all, the fast-food chain has undergone a clever transition in terms of image and assortment towards healthier eating, as it faced increasing pressure from the growing problem of obesity in the Western world. In its visual identity, it has therefore swapped the colours of red and yellow, strongly associated with fast food, in favour of dark green and yellow. And McDonalds, always known for having the same assortment in every branch, now adapts part of its assortment to reflect national cuisine. In the Netherlands there is the McKroket and a McFlurry syrup waffle, McDonalds offers McHalal for Muslims and McPork in Japan. And in China, as well as children's parties, you can also celebrate your wedding in McDonalds.

Kbane is a French DIY store focusing on healthy, ecological and environmentally-friendly living. The store is as sustainable as possible too.

ACTIVATING THE BRAND

IF THE CUSTOMER IS TO COME FIRST, IT IS NECESSARY TO REACH, INFORM AND ASSIST HIM OR HER WHEREVER THAT MAY BE. THANKS TO THE INCREASING USE OF MOBILE INTERNET, IT IS NOW MUCH EASIER TO REACH THE CUSTOMER WHILST OUT AND ABOUT.

This is making retail omni-channel: throughout the sales process, from awareness and orientation to actual purchase, different channels are increasingly being used alongside each other and in combination, at different times and places. Research conducted into cross-channel retail by the Dutch bank ABN-Amro has revealed that exclusively online or exclusively off-line shopping is set to decline. Nowadays, people are often pre-prepared when they set off and this makes them shop more efficiently: rather than spending the whole day drifting through town, they specifically target a number of stores, planned in advance. The social media generation has a different way of shopping and retail must respond to this. More and more, the customer journey is becoming an important part of the retail brand. Strong brands can increasingly gain a presence as a platform that can engage in interaction with consumers at a range of different moments.

The Platform Development Model© is the container for the retail formula, consisting of all the retail elements, nourished by the brand identity.

Through the interplay of all these elements, the brand ambitions are aspired to. But what else can be done in order to follow up on these ambitions? The scope of the brand and the ambitions can be shaped by using the Brand in Your Hand Model©, a brainstorming tool for creatively shaping the relationship and brand/customer meeting places. The model can be used to investigate how to mould the future of the retail brand and how to make the brand into a platform. In this, innovation, brand activation and differentiation are key principles.

■ *In the relationship between the brand and consumers, the brand must reveal its face. The personality of the brand is important. At its entrances, Dutch supermarket 'Landmarkt' displays the faces of its local farmer partners.*

212

■ *Platform Development Model©.*

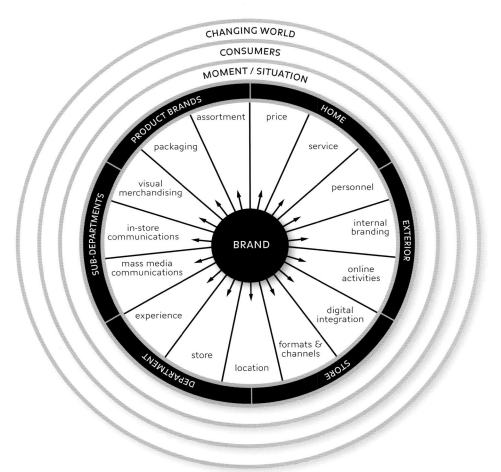

213

Although not originally a retailer, Jamie Oliver is without doubt a strong and versatile brand: here is a man with a mission, which he applies widely. The way he has made himself into a brand and continually developed his formula is a perfect illustration of the Brand in Your Hand Model©.

Jamie Oliver aspires to bring good and tasty food to as many people as possible. He started out with various, innovative cookery programmes in which he shows you how you can make healthy and tasty food relatively easily. In this, he presented himself as a pleasant and charismatic person. He shows where he gets his inspiration from, who his gurus are and at which markets he buys his fresh produce. He is also open about his own life: the London life he enjoys, his relationship and his friends. All of this quickly made Jamie Oliver into a real brand personality representing a lifestyle to which many people aspired.

This lifestyle created numerous options for expanding his brand. If one had to name Jamie Oliver's brand values, they might be quality, honesty and passion. His aim is to motivate people and make tasty cooking accessible. His ambition is to help as many people as possible to eat better food and live better lives. Based on this market definition, he has found plenty of space in which to develop his brand in multiple ways.

A logical follow-up to his cookery programmes was to publish cookbooks featuring the recipes from his programmes. But his ambition has also enabled him to develop many more products and services that match his brand. He clearly pursues an omni-channel strategy and has actually developed himself as a platform. In alliance with licensing partners, he markets a range of cooking equipment and accessories in his name, designed to make cooking more convenient, such as a pan set and barbecue equipment. But he has also developed his own kitchenware and markets a range of different pasta sauces. He has opened numerous restaurant chains, including Jamie's Italian, a version of the Italian Dolce Vita.

Through these restaurants, he aims to be at the centre of the local community, inspired by the big Italian table where people come together and enjoy tasty food. The Recipease stores are a similar concept to this restaurant chain: they offer special workshops (food parties), tips from the chef and ready-made dishes for sale. He aims to encourage people to experiment with food and try out new recipes more often. But he has extended his formula even further, by becoming the face of the Sainsbury's supermarket chain, emphasizing the importance of healthy eating in a series of TV commercials. He has also developed apps and videos for mobile telephones with recipes in text and on video.

■ *Jamie Oliver's Union Jack, just before opening.*

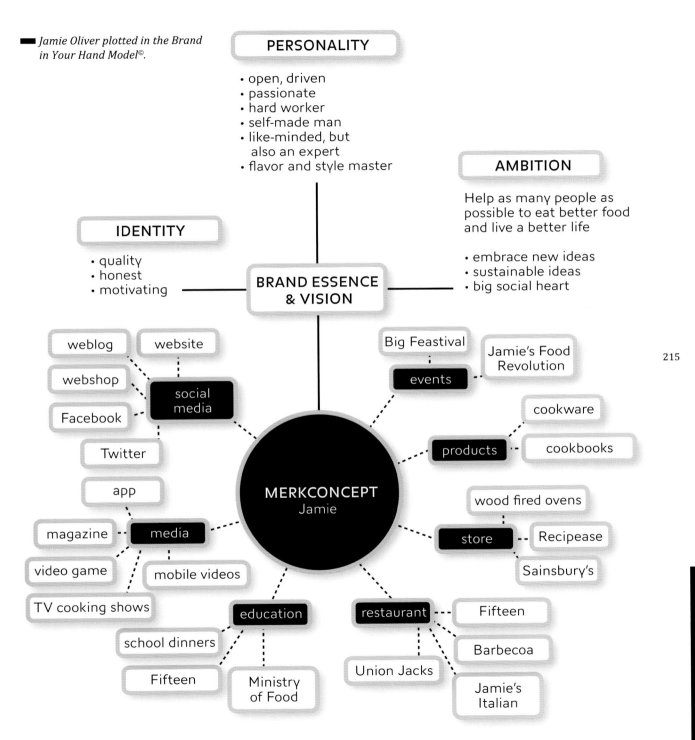

Jamie Oliver plotted in the Brand in Your Hand Model©.

PERSONALITY
- open, driven
- passionate
- hard worker
- self-made man
- like-minded, but also an expert
- flavor and style master

AMBITION

Help as many people as possible to eat better food and live a better life

- embrace new ideas
- sustainable ideas
- big social heart

IDENTITY
- quality
- honest
- motivating

BRAND ESSENCE & VISION

MERKCONCEPT
Jamie

social media
- weblog
- website
- webshop
- Facebook

media
- Twitter
- app
- magazine
- video game
- mobile videos
- TV cooking shows

education
- school dinners
- Fifteen
- Ministry of Food

restaurant
- Fifteen
- Barbecoa
- Union Jacks
- Jamie's Italian

store
- wood fired ovens
- Recipease
- Sainsbury's

products
- cookware
- cookbooks

events
- Big Feastival
- Jamie's Food Revolution

He even stars in a videogame in which he explains how to cook and all about healthy eating.

Jamie Oliver's ambition inspires him to be even more active in bringing people into contact with good food. He also deliberately targets people who are less affluent. He started the restaurant concept, Fifteen, which trains deprived youngsters in all aspects of working in a restaurant. He has campaigned to bring better food to children in British schools. The 'Jamie's School Dinners' project featured on its own TV series and depicts his revolutionary ambition to confront parents and children with the fact that they are not eating enough healthy food. He has even involved the government by asking them to increase subsidies for school meals and to change the school canteen system.

Jamie Oliver has developed his brand extremely widely. However, because he made his identity and ambitions extremely clear from the outset, the consumer understands the origin of these brand activities. Everything he does, is based on his brand and reflects what he excels in. But to achieve this, it is also important to understand the market and consumers well. Of course, the sector in which he works is extremely wide: cooking, cookbooks and cooking equipment have an obvious and logical connection. His ambition offers multiple possibilities, but he has handled it well, always carefully controlling his brand and taking account of his brand image. In that respect, Jamie Oliver also has a business mentality. All ideas are assessed in terms of the brand principles. These have been laid down in a brand guide, in order to ensure that it becomes a proper brand

and is not too dependent on him as a person. The brand needs to stand on its own feet and continue to exist, which is why it also works according to the franchise principle. He always ensures that quality is good and therefore works only with the best people and partners.

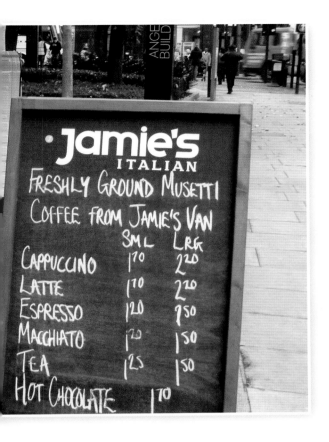

■ *Top left: one of Jamie Oliver's restaurants is Jamie's Italian. Italy is the inspiration for his cooking.*

Top right: Jamie Oliver's cookbooks feature on many a bookcase.

Below: the workshop area in Jamie Oliver's Recipease.

10. THE COMPLEXITY OF RETAIL

CONSISTENCY AND COHERENCE

**BY DEVELOPING AND EFFECTIVELY IMPLE-
MENTING A WIDE-RANGING NUMBER OF
CUSTOMER CONTACT POINTS, AS JAMIE
OLIVER DOES, YOU CAN DEVELOP A MORE
ACTIVE AND STRONGER BRAND, WHILST
SIMULTANEOUSLY SPREADING RISK: THE
WIDE SUPPORT AND RANGE OF BRAND
ACTIVITIES GIVES YOU ROOM TO MANOEU-
VRE IN THE MARKET, TO EVOLVE WITH THE
SPIRIT OF THE AGE AND CHANGES IN ITS
CONTEXT.**

WWhatever happens, retail will change. This is
something we have tried to emphasize in this
book. But what will always stay the same, in ten
years' time or even beyond, is the one-to-one relationship between the consumer and the retailer,
because this has been the essence of retail since
time immemorial. It just needs to be continually
reshaped in new, contemporary, relevant and
unique ways. If that is achieved, the retailer retains the right to exist and it matters little in what
form or place it happens. Consistency and coherence in all the points of contact with the retail
concept are essential in order that the customer
recognizes and understands it wherever he has
contact with the retail brand.

It seems that a consistent and coherent concept
is not only becoming increasingly important for
the store, but also for the high street and the
shopping centre. The success of the high street
is under threat, because of the pressure of time
we face, (we are increasingly less likely to take
the time to go through the whole high street)
increasing problems with access to the retail
area, the growing role of the internet, the ageing
population and recession. The relentless spread
of chain stores means that high streets and shopping centres are becoming increasingly identical.
In whichever town or city you are, you will find
more or less the same offering. This is an important factor in making shopping areas increasingly
empty. As the high street becomes more generic, its added value diminishes and other sales
locations become more interesting. Why would
you go shopping with friends in Amsterdam or
London, if you can find the same things on offer
in your local shopping centre? It makes your day
less exciting, less special, if you do not have to
go to a particular, fun city. Shopping becomes a
chore instead of fun. And why take the trouble to

Westfield shopping centre in London.

buy particular products in a shopping area (with limited and expensive parking), if you can order it online in an instant?

Local councils are increasingly deploying city marketing in order to showcase the strengths and distinctive value of their city among its residents, visitors and retailers. This is always based on a clear proposition. After all, an effective experience and concept are the added values that will encourage all of us to head out en masse. When the international shopping centre brand Westfield opened its second location in London, Europe's largest shopping centre with 250 stores and 70 restaurants, it attracted as many as

200,000 visitors on its first day alone. After six days, this figure had reached 1 million! This was despite the fact that this shopping centre was not even 10 km from the first London Westfield. The power of Westfield is that it maintains effective control over the retailers that wish to set up business in the shopping centre. First of all, the retailers must submit their plans and store concept for approval. This ensures that the shopping centre's concept and image remain under control and a high standard is set, with the result that all retailers open their very best stores here. This is one way of creating value. Westfield has also carefully assessed its location and catchment area enabling it to provide a suitable offering to the customer groups it expects. In the shopping centre itself, various different worlds have been created featuring retailers that match the target groups: there are the usual high street brands like Primark and Forever21, but also designer brands such as Prada and Tag Heuer. Additional services are also on offer, including a massage parlour, an extensive cloakroom (where you can also leave your shopping!), a cinema and a range of catering establishments, ensuring that shoppers can have a relaxed day out. Because Westfield fully understands the essence of retail and acts accordingly, it is successful, with at least 25 million visitors expected each year and turnover reaching £1 billion.

Even shopping areas need to keep close control of their concept and strengths.

Even small-scale shopping areas can be a success if they keep careful control of their concept and strengths. London's Camden Town is a popular area of this kind as are the Nine Streets (Negen Straatjes) in Amsterdam. This mainly includes small boutiques, where the retailers share responsibility for maintenance and development. This initiative can also be seen in the virtual version of this retail area, 9straatjes.nl, a webshop offering the products of affiliated retailers. It is the uniqueness and variation of the retail offering here that makes the Negen Straatjes so great and provides the added value for visitors. However, increasing numbers of chain stores are gradually moving in here, albeit with their very best con-

cept, because they want to take advantage of this successful area and reach its customers. But if the retailers do not continue to set high standards, this could result in the dilution of the concept of the area, which could then deteriorate into just any other shopping street.

Developments in Fifth Avenue in New York City were dubbed by the New York Post as 'the mallification of the shopping street'. This was originally home exclusively to leading designer brands, who were able to afford the exorbitant rents in the heart of this prosperous area. But now, mainstream brands are increasingly opening up business, such as Uniqlo, Zara, Abercrombie & Fitch, Hollister, H&M and Gap. Still, it cannot be argued that this has made the retail image more generic, since the retailers are basing what they call their statement stores at this top location. These aim to offer the very best experience and introduction to all aspects of the brand: a marketing tool in the world's most popular shopping street, which is worth the enormous rent.

As the Platform Development Model© shows, a retail formula exists in its own context. On the one hand, this is made up of influences at macro-level, but the retail brand must never forget the local context. Ultimately, the location of the store will also have a major influence on the mindset of the consumer, the store and how it is perceived. The location is part of the positioning and success of the store. In order to have control over that, it is advisable to work in close cooperation with surrounding retailers in order to project a clear and distinctive proposition together: global branding, local marketing. But often, chains lack the necessary flexibility to adapt to the specific location and visitor if they are managed from head office, leading to the threat of increasing uniformity and

Fifth Avenue in New York. This photo clearly
shows the stunning Louis Vuitton store.

221

10. THE COMPLEXITY OF RETAIL

monotony. Ideally, the head office will work to increase national and global brand recognition and provide service support to the stores. It is then up to those at local level to anticipate the needs of the specific surroundings. Starbucks is now beginning to respond in this way. For example, Starbucks, which is now on almost every corner with its familiar, but uniform, third-place concept, is now developing a local concept that adapts to the specific location. On 15th Avenue in New York, it has opened a cafe with the appropriate name 15th Avenue Coffee & Tea. In terms of look & feel, the concept is not recognizably Starbucks, but under the logo are the words 'inspired by Starbucks'. In Japan, Starbucks has a branch that primarily seems to be a design statement. Japanese architects designed the cafe using 2000 wooden slats.

222

In order to make a success of a high street or shopping centre, it should actually be treated as if it were a retail formula according to the Platform Development Model©, in which all the elements are connected and work together. This creates a clear concept and the mix of retailers can then be included in the model. A combination of major retailers and great independent retailers results in a variation that shoppers are looking for: an one-stop shopping experience. By alternating with catering facilities, you can also ensure that shoppers can recharge their batteries before more retail therapy. You can also include entertainment in the form of fashion shows, concerts and events. This provides even more added value to shoppers. Another concept that shopping consumers appreciate is 2theloo: 'toilet shops' in city centres, shopping centres, railway stations and petrol stations. 2theloo was inspired by the problem that even in the busiest places it is difficult to find a clean toilet. This is despite the fact that these

A retailformula exists in its own context. The local context should not be forgotten, because the location has a lot of influence on the mindset of the consumer.

■ *Left: the small-scale retail district 'The 9 Streets' in Amsterdam.*

Right: 'Toilet retailer' 2TheLoo in the Kalverstraat in Amsterdam.

are exactly the places where you need one. Even here, the target group was taken into account: for parents with children, there is a family toilet and there is an adapted toilet for people with a disability. Next to the toilets, there is a store selling toilet products, a cloakroom and sometimes a coffee corner.

Let us be clear: generic stores, high streets and shopping centres need to continue to develop. Going to a physical store is no longer a matter of course: it has become a choice. You can now get things anywhere, even on the internet: the key is to add value. This is what makes people come to you. Cor Molenaar puts it this way: physical retail is now competing with the internet and the living room. Shopping centres need to be so relevant and fun that people prefer to be there than at home.

Ultimately, in the store and in the retail area, it is all about seduction: seducing people to go in and to go through the whole street or store. The consumer needs to be inquisitive enough to do that and that calls for variety and surprises. And if all the retail elements are right, you will have a strong concept with which you can seduce the consumer and fulfil his needs again and again.

224

The ultimate seduction at Abercrombie & Fitch, people stand in line to enter the store and feature on the photo with staff, as shown here in London.

"Physical retail is now competing with the internet and the living room. Shopping centres need to be so relevant and fun that people prefer to be there than at home."

COR MOLENAAR
IN 'THE END OF SHOPS?'

IF YOU DON'T KNOW WHERE YOU'RE GOING, ANY ROAD WILL TAKE YOU THERE

A FINAL WORD

Some people love brands and find them a support of their ego, others find brands manipulative, false absurdities, which are invented by the commercial world. Probably, they both are right, but even for people who are suspicious about branding, brands are auxiliaries in the immense world of decisions that we have to make per day, week or every once in a while. About the food that we buy in the supermarket, the shop where we want to go to for a new winter coat, and even about the political parties that we should vote for. Brands help to define ourselves, who we are and how we want to be seen. We think about brands as acquaintances, friends, or even enemies. We have preferences, disapprovals and sometimes we have no interest at all. Brands give direction and help to achieve your ambitions: the dream of owning a Jaguar once, to the goals to join Greenpeace. Brands are personifications; a little is created by the owner, a little by the spectators and a bit by yourself. Partly, a brand can be appointed, but the rest is mystical, it is 'somewhere in the air'.

If a brand gives direction, the brand must have a direction itself. The brand must have a purpose or several: long term, short term, a commercial purpose, but also some higher ambition. "If you do not know where you're going, any road will take you there," wrote George Harrison in 1988. It was a free interpretation of a conversation between Alice and the Chesire Cat from 'Alice in Wonderland'. Alice asked the cat if he wanted to be so kind to tell her which way to go. "That depends a great deal on where you want to go," he said. "I do not really care," Alice had replied. "Then it does not matter which way you go," said the cat. "If I get *somewhere* at least," Alice had explained to him. "Oh, you're certainly going to succeed in that," said the cat, "if you walk long enough." This is about objectives and strategies, but it also gives the understanding that if you do nothing, you will get somewhere. Although it might be the abyss.

Brands and people: they are intertwined. And if you have something (if only a little bit) with people, – which is useful if you work in retail –, then there is little better than to be occupied with that. And with the future of course, because that is there we go.

Michel van Tongeren.

230

BIBLIOGRAPHY

ABN AMRO & CBW MITEX (2011). *De consument van 2015: Cross channel retail.* Consulted on 2011, November 21 via http://www.cbwmitex. nl/pages/1559/Webshops-verliezen-terrein.html (in Dutch)

BISHOP, S. & CHO, D. (2008, spring). *From plague to paradigma: Designing sustainable environments.* In Rotman Magazine.

BOUTEN, L. (2010). *Co-Branding: A brand partnership and a new product.* Doctoral thesis: University of Technology Delft.

BROWN, T. (2009, first edition). *Change by design: How design thinking creates new alternatives for business and society.* New York: HarperCollins Publishers Inc.

CHAZIN, S. (2007). *Marketing Apple: 5 secrets of the world's best marketing machine.* Consulted on 2010, March 10 via http://www.marketingapple. com/.

CLAWSON, T. (2010, first edition). *The unauthorized guide tot doing business the Jamie Oliver way: 10 secrets of the represaille one man brand.* West Sussex: Capstone Publishing Ltd.

COLLINS, K. (2009, first edition). *Watching what we eat: The evolution of television cooking shows.* London: Continuum.

DE BOTTON, A. (2005). *Status Anxiety.* New York: Viking Penguin.

FITCH, R. & KNOBEL, L. (1990, first edition). *Fitch on retail design.* Oxford, Phaidon Press Limited.

FLEMING, K. (2011, December 17). *Taking the Fifth, How chain stores turned NYC's most glamorous avenue into America's glitziest mall.* In New York Post.

GIANOTTEN, H. (2001, January). *Het creëren van klantwaarde.* In Detailhandel Magazine. (in Dutch)

GODIN, S. (2010, first edition). *Linchpin: Are you indispensable?* New York: Penguin Group USA.

HAMEL, G. & PRAHALAD, C.K. (1994). *Competing for the future.* Boston: Harvard Business Press.

HAWKINS STRATEGIC LLC. (2009). *The Retail 3.0 organization.* Consulted on 2010, February 10 via http://hawkinsstrategic.com/hs/ Retail_3.0.html.

INTERBRAND (2012). *Best Retail Brands.* Consulted on 2012, February 21 via http://interbrand.com/nl/BestRetailBrands/2012-Best-Retail-Brands.aspx.

HEEG, R. (2011, October 28). *Op zoek naar je innerlijke merk.* In Adformatie, 39, nr. 43, pp. 38-39. (in Dutch)

JENSEN, S. (2011, May 31). *Koken is net als klussen – eerlijk, authentiek en sexy.* In NRC Next, pp. 12. (in Dutch)

JUDITH, A. (2004, reprinted). *Eastern Body, Western Mind : Psychology and the Chakra System as a Path to the Self.* Berkeley: Celestial Arts.

KOTLER, PH. (2010, first edition). *Marketing 3.0.* Den Haag: Academic Service.

LAO TSE & HAMILL. S. (2006, October). *Tao Te Tsjing.* Amsterdam: Samsara Uitgeverij B.V.

LEVITT, T. (1983). *Globalization of markets.* In Harvard Business Review, 1983, May/June, pp 92-102.

LINZMAYER, O. (2004, second edition). *Apple Confidential 2.0: The definitive history of the world's most colorful company.* San Francisco: No Starch Press.

MICHELS, W. & MICHELS, Y. (2011, first edition). *Focus op fans: Het boek over brandactivation.* Zaltbommel: Thema. (in Dutch)

MOLENAAR, C. (2010, first edition). *Shopping 3.0: Shopping, the Internet or both.* Hampshire: Gower Publishing Limited.

O'CASS, A. & GRACE, D. (2008, May 8). *Understanding the role of retail store service in the light of self-image – store-image congruence.* In Psychology & Marketing, 25, nr. 6, pp. 521-537.
NIEUWENHUIS, M. (2003, second edition). *The art of management, deel 1: strategie en structuur.* Amsterdam: The art of management. (in Dutch)
NIJS, D. & PETERS, F. (2002, first edition). *Imagineering: het creëren van belevingswerelden.* Den Haag: Boom Lemma Uitgevers. (in Dutch)
OLINS, W. (1999, reprinted). *The new guide to identity.* Hampshire: Gower Publishing Limited.
PINE, J. & GILMORE, J. (1999, first edition). *The experience economy.* Boston: Harvard Business School Press.
PORTER, M. (1997, July/August). *How competitive forces shape strategy.* In Harvard Business Review.
PROJECT ON THE CITY 2 (2001, first edition). *Harvard Design School Guide to Shopping.* Keulen: Taschen.
QUIX, F. & VAN DER KIND, R. (2012, fifth edition). *Retailmarketing.* Groningen: Noordhoff Uitgevers. (in Dutch)
RIEZEBOS, R. & VAN DER GRINTEN, J. (2011, second edition). *Postioneren: Stappenplan voor een scherpe positionering.* Den Haag: Boom Lemma Uitgevers. (in Dutch)
RIJKENBERG, J. (2001, fifth edition). *Concepting, Het managen van Concept-merken in het communicatiegeoriënteerde tijdperk.* Den Haag: Uitgever BZZTôH. (in Dutch)
ROBERTS, K. (2004). *Lovemarks: The future beyond brands.* New York: powerHouse Books.
SMIT, R. (2010, July 20). *Beter ontworpen product laat de kassa rinkelen.* In Het Financieele Dagblad, pp. 9. (in Dutch)
SPIRID. (2008). *Onderzoek naar vrouwelijke versus mannelijke waarden.* (in Dutch)

STIENSTRA, J. (2010, March 20). *Mythes in marketing, stop mensen niet zomaar in een hokje.* In Het Financieele Dagblad, pp. 17. (in Dutch)
STOLZE, J. (2011, first edition). *Uitverkocht! Welkom in de aandachtseconomie.* Utrecht: A.W. Bruna. (in Dutch)
THE INTEGER GROUP. (2009). *Shopper vs. Consumer: communication to shifting mindsets.* Consulted on 2009 February 16 via http://www.shopperculture.com/shopper_culture/white-papers.html.
THOMASSEN, L., LINCOLN, K. & ACONIS, A. (2009, first edition). *Retailization: Brand survival in the age of retailer power.* London: Kogan Page.
TILLEY, A. & HENRY DREYFUSS ASSOCIATES. (2002, second revised edition). *The measure of man and woman: Human factors in design.* Hoboken: John Wiley and Sons Ltd.
TREACY, M. & WIERSEMA, F. (1997, expanded edition). *The discipline of market leaders: Choose your customers, narrow your focus, dominate your market.* New York: Basic Books.
UNDERHILL, P. (1999). *Why we buy: The science of shopping.* New York: Simon & Schuster.
VAN DER LOO, H., GEELHOED, J. & SAMHOUD, S. (2010, fifth edition). *Kus de visie wakker: Organisaties energiek en effectief maken.* Den Haag: Academic Service. (in Dutch)
VAN DER ZWAAL, J. (2000, second edition). *Design voor opdrachtgevers.* Amsterdam: Bis Publishers. (in Dutch)
VAN DONGEN, B. (2010, March 30). In Marketingtribune, 27, nr. 6, pp. 17. (in Dutch)
VAN ESVELD, W. (2010, March 30). *Pleidooi voor designmanagement.* In Marketingtribune, 27, nr. 6, pp. 10-12. (in Dutch)
VAN KRALINGEN, R. (2003, first edition). *Superbrands: Merken en markten van morgen.* Den Haag: Kluwer. (in Dutch)

VAN LIER, B. (2010, March 25). *Design in euro's.* In Adformatie, 38, nr. 12, pp. 32-33. (in Dutch)

VAN MIERLO, J. (2011, October 3). *Nieuw Londens winkelwalhalla mikt op 25 miljoen betalende bezoekers per jaar.* In Het Financieele Dagblad, pp. 11. (in Dutch)

VAN SCHEERDIJK, H. (2010). *RMC Visie: Online versus offline shoppen: waarom de retailer in de winkelstraat sterk staat in deze strijd.* Consulted on 2010 February 24 via retailactueel.com/ r2460/Online-versus-offline-shoppen%3B- waarom-de-retailer-in-de-winkelstraat-sterk- staat-in-deze-strijd. (in Dutch)

VAN WOENSEL KOOY, P. (2010, March 30). *Internal branding 3.0.* In Marketingtribune, 27, nr. 6, pp. 26-27. (in Dutch)

VERHEIJEN, T. (2010, March). *Ongeslepen diamanten.* In Emerce, pp. 36-40. (in Dutch)

VERMEYLEN, S. (2005, second edition). *Werken met de SWOT-analyse.* Brussel: Politeia. (in Dutch)

WALVIS, T. (2008). *Three laws of branding: neuroscientific foundations of effective brand building.* In Journal of Brand Management, 16, pp. 176-194.

WIJMAN, E. (2011, July 8). *'Klanten willen dansen'.* In Adformatie, 39, nr. 27-28, pp. 22-25. (in Dutch)

ZEC, P. & BURKHARD, J. (2011). *Design value: a strategy for business success.* Ludwigsburg: Avedition Gmbh.

Action wil sneller groeien zonder poespas. (2012, January 29). Consulted on 2012, February 2 via http://www.supplychainmagazine.nl/action-wil- sneller-groeien-zonder-poespas/. (in Dutch)

Gestalt. Consulted on 2012, April 20 via http:// en.wikipedia.org/wiki/Gestalt_psychology

Man is the measure of all things. Consulted on 2012, April 20 via http://en.wikipedia.org/wiki/ Protagoras.

Maslow's hierarchy of needs. Consulted on 2012 April 13 via http://en.wikipedia.org/wiki/ Maslow%27s_hierarchy_of_needs

Van bezit naar toegang en ervaring. (2011, 23 februari). In NRC Next, pp. 3. (in Dutch)

WEBSITES
- 2theloo.com
- Adformatie.nl
- CreatejobsfortheUSA.com
- Hbd.nl
- Ikea.com
- Marketingtribune.nl
- Mystarbucksidea.com
- Nespresso.com
- Retailnews.nl
- Retailactueel.nl
- Rmc.nl
- Starbucks.com
- Supplychainmagazine.nl
- Trendwatching.com
- VSDM.com
- Geheugenvannederland.nl
- De9straatjes.nl

233

234

MODELS

URE **SHOULD BE TAKEN** SERIOUSLY

Charles Eames

237

THE ESSENCE OF RETAIL IS THE ONE TO ONE RELATIONSHIP BETWEEN COMPANIES AND REAL PEOPLE.